MIRROR MIRROR

MIRROR MIRROR
What Reflection Do You See?

ADRIENE BRYANT WRIGHT, PH.D., PCLC

ABELITA PRESS

Unless otherwise indicated, all Scripture quotations are from the *ESV Bible* (*The Holy Bible, English Standard Version*), copyright © 2001 by Crossway, a publishing ministry of Good News Publishers. Used by permission. All rights reserved.

Scripture taken from *The Message*. Copyright © 1993, 1994, 1995, 1996, 2000, 2001, 2002. Used by permission of NavPress Publishing Group.

Scripture taken from the New King James Version. Copyright © 1982 by Thomas Nelson. Used by permission. All rights reserved.
Scriptures marked (KJV) are taken from the King James Version (KJV), public domain.

Scripture quotations marked (NIV) are taken from the *Holy Bible*, New International Version, NIV. Copyright © 1973, 1978, 1984, 2011 by Biblica, Inc.™ Used by permission of Zondervan. All rights reserved worldwide. www.zondervan.com The "NIV" and "New International Version" are trademarks registered in the United States Patent and Trademark Office by Biblica, Inc.™

Copyright Registration with the U.S. Library of Congress 2013: ISBN 978-0-9899041-0-0
All rights reserved

Cover Design by Lisa Hainline, Lionsgate Book Design
Interior layout by Steven Plummer, SPBookDesign
Contributing Editor, Glyndell B. Presley

Published by Abelita Press
www.abelita.org
Printed in the United States of America

Acknowledgments

I GIVE SPECIAL ACKNOWLEDGEMENT to my daughters, Chloé Saint Claire and Ariel Nicole Tinker, who provided the inspiration and idea for this writing. Thank you, Chloé, for applying your command of the English language, grammar and punctuation in the editing of this book and Ariel, for your gentle but unrelenting push to finish the book.

I am so thankful for the many friends and prayer partners that believed in me but moreover, believed in what God is doing through me. I especially acknowledge my friend, publishing coach and mentor, Mary Katherine Ard'is who openly shared her experience and expertise in writing and publishing.

While there are many who offered prayers, encouragement and inspiration, I give a special acknowledgement in loving memory of Mother Clarice Bryant who demonstrated through her life that we can live as examples of Jesus Christ.

Table of Contents

Preface ix

Chapter 1 A Personal Reflection. 1

Chapter 2 The Mirror and Reflection! 9

Chapter 3 Your Slip Is Hanging! 31

Chapter 4 Validation Addiction 45

Chapter 5 Situational Ethics. 53

Chapter 6 A Clash of Cultures. 67

Chapter 7 A Looking Glass for Others. 79

Chapter 8 A Righteous Standard 89

Chapter 9 To Mirror God Is to Know God. 101

Chapter 10 A Righteous Reflection .119

Chapter 11 The Broken Mirror 129

Chapter 12 Be All In 145

Chapter 13 The New Norm: Exposed 153

Preface

MIRRORS ARE COMMON here in the United States. They are in our homes, in the workplace, in public restrooms and in our retail shops. They appear to be everywhere, and we use them regularly. While we are constantly examining our external appearance, do we ever pause to examine our internal being? Do we check our attitude, or moral values, or our character?

1 Corinthians 11:28 tells us that we must examine ourselves. 2 Corinthians 13:5 further tells us that we are to both test and examine ourselves to see if we are in the faith. While we may look in the mirror every day, we may not have a full understanding of how we are to examine ourselves. We have our own interpretation and understanding of what is acceptable or unacceptable. We set our own standards and choose our own role models to emulate and we mimic the behaviors we like and admire. While at the same time, it appears that we are unaware that we are also examples for others. There are others who mimic what they see in us whether it is good behavior or bad behavior. There are others that may be following in our example but is it the

example that we really want others to emulate? A question that will be repeatedly asked in this book is, "What reflection do you see?"

Over the course of my journey with Christ, I have often thought there was nothing more within me to clean up or clean out, only to discover something new. Sometimes, old things returned and needed to be addressed again. This time, more deeply and more completely. Sometimes, it was a slow and gradual process. There were times when transformation took place in one area that opened another area. Each time, I became more aware that no matter how close I thought I was getting to perfection, there was always room for improvement.

There is a transformational process that begins when we acknowledge and submit to Jesus Christ as our Lord and Savior. It is through his divinity that he knows our eternal being, purpose, and destiny. It is through his humanity that he fully understands the daily war that we fight with our flesh; sin, sickness, disease, sorrow, and suffering. It is through his intercession for us to the Father that we are enabled to be more like Him. It is through this spiritual and experiential transformation that we become beneficiaries of our heavenly Father's constant and daily outpouring of mercy and grace.

The transformational process is a lifelong commitment to Christ, his teachings, his authority, his divinity as the soon-and-coming King, and the belief that he is the Messiah. Our human aspirations and achievements cannot compare with our relationship with Christ. Our relationship with Christ is much more than just placing a check mark next to the act of reciting the sinner's prayer, and baptism. While there are many self-help books on the market today, there are none more compelling or thorough than a spiritual transformation through Christ Jesus.

My highest aim for this book is to provide insight into the reflection we see. It examines what others see, what God sees, and what we should aspire to see in ourselves. This writing uses scriptural and biblical perspectives of how we are to examine ourselves and experience a greater understanding of the transformational process in our lifelong Christian journey.

There have been and continue to be many role models in my life. These are phenomenal individuals: men and women of great faith who have experienced transformation and are now discipling others. Their inner strength, faith, and confident demeanor, regardless of the circumstances they encounter, have been a formidable testimony to me that God is not only able, but faithful, to not leave us amid calamity. I have observed the longevity of a life of quality by not just existing, but actively living and being engaged.

Most importantly, I have found that those who are continually being transformed are impacting the kingdom of God in their homes, families, communities, and workplaces, and are making a difference, globally. These are not "special" people with fancy titles, positions, or even talents. They are simply ordinary people who have a pure heart for God, who hear his voice, who follow his commands, willingly trust in his way, and abide in his presence. These are people like David, the shepherd boy, whom nobody respected, but who became a great king. The Word describes him as "a man after God's own heart." Joseph was also an ordinary boy, sold into slavery by his brothers. He did not abandon God, nor did God abandon him in his incarceration. Through the humble beginnings of transformation, God's plan yet prevailed. Moses was also transformed by God, before embarking on the greatest assignment of his life. His destiny was to deliver God's chosen people from slavery and bondage, to a land flowing with milk and honey.

Do you know God's plan for your life? What is your destiny and life's purpose? It is in the transformation process that we come to develop a oneness with God. It is in our pursuit of God that, not only do we grow more into His image and likeness, but we get closer and closer to Him. We too can experience what Paul describes in 1 Corinthians 2:9, "But as it is written, eye hath not seen, nor ear heard, neither have entered into the heart of man, the things which God hath prepared for them that love him."

It is my prayer that each reader can through these writings, gain a greater awareness of God's divine plan that is rooted in the transformational process. This process begins by facing the mirror and seeing our own unique and individual reflection. Are you ready?

Introduction

IT HAS BEEN an observation of mine for many years that there are many who speak the language of Christianity and claim to be Christians, but appear to display little evidence of the nature, character, or likeness of Christ Jesus. While I recognize that none of us are perfect, nor will we ever be in these mortal bodies, how can we be all that God has created us to be without transformation? Paul illustrates this in Hebrews 5:12, where he describes some who have been believers for a while and should have become disciples and teachers, but are sadly, still immature and can only understand the basic things about God's word. "You need milk, not solid food" (ESV).

Believers are bombarded by images of immorality that dominate radio and television airways, the Internet and print. Our minds are saturated with the lyrics of songs that range from indifference and vanity to obscenity. There is a belief by some, that if the American public is bombarded with shocking ideologies and images that the initial reaction may be one of shock, but with continual displays, become desensitized and then complacent. They are no longer outraged, or even moved, but begin to see it as, 'a way of life'. This way of life can challenge our moral values. Have you experienced a continual pressure to conform to worldly influences and projected images of what is considered to be acceptable? Godly values are compromised and supplanted by modern-day perspectives. The family structure as we have always known is supplanted with an alternate structure. Visceral debates over human sexuality are the focal points in local and national elections. Some have poignantly asked, "Where is God?" or question whether God exists, due to many atrocities occurring in the world.

As believers, we know that there is a God who is omnipresent and omniscient. As believers, we are called to be as children of the light and reflect that which we call ourselves—Christians. Isn't it time that we begin to live in such a way that no verbal confession is really needed? Shouldn't the world see that we are those who seek after Christ and exemplify his teachings, not through lip service or preaching, but by our godly character and nature? Isn't it time that we, as Christians, stop adopting worldly ideologies, but be transformed into the image and likeness of Christ? If we call ourselves Christians, then isn't it time that we begin to show Christ Jesus in our everyday lives?

This message being put forward in this writing is that far too many within the Body of Christ are not reaching their fullest potential and circumvent the plans and purposes that God has for them. Some would rather choose a pathway of self-indulgence. Some have become accustomed to doing things their way to get what they desire, as opposed to submitting to God and trusting that he will provide blessings and direction in life to fulfill his plan. While this writing discusses some elements of present-day Christendom in America, the emphasis of this writing is about the inner self, and its silent impact on others.

Those claiming to be believers or disciples of Christ have become ineffective in setting forth a true example of Jesus Christ, due to an inner reflection that casts more profoundly. This writing is to sound the alarm that it is time for all of those who profess Christianity, whether new to Christianity, or maturing saints, to rise up and become new creatures in Christ Jesus as the Bibles teaches us in 2 Corinthians 5:17: *"Therefore, if anyone is in Christ, he is a new creation; old things have passed away; behold, all things have become new." (NKJV)*. We must, both individually and corporately as the Church, stand before the mirror and examine ourselves (1 Corinthians 11:31) in comparison to the life and teachings of our Lord Jesus Christ. We must examine individual behaviors, and moral values. It is not enough to only talk about our beliefs. We must also demonstrate them by the way we live and how we interact with others. We only deceive ourselves when we do so. James 1:23-24 tells us:

> *"Do not merely listen to the word, and so deceive yourselves. Do what it says. Anyone who listens to the word but does not do what it says is like a man who looks at his face in a mirror and, after looking at himself, goes away and immediately forgets what he looks like."*

We know that no human shall ever, in these mortal bodies, reach a state of perfection in this life. Nonetheless, it is upon us as Christians and disciples of Christ to live holy and righteous lives and serve as an example of Christ Jesus to others. It requires constant focus. Perhaps it is like how I get dressed in the morning for work. I pay close attention to my hair and makeup. But as I go through the day, I am rarely attentive to these things until I go the ladies room and look in the mirror. My hair does not always stay in place and my makeup requires "touch-ups." Our walk with Christ is like that. We must continually be mindful of our relationship, the transformative process and what it means to be a Disciple of Christ.

This writing is for those who seek to thrive by living a fulfilled and purposeful life that God has designed. It begins with examining ourselves and embracing the spirit of truth in every aspect of our life. A most profound question that is asked throughout this book is:

What Reflection Do You See?

Chapter 1
A Personal Reflection

I would like to buy $3 worth of God, please—not enough to explode my soul or disturb my sleep, but just enough to equal a cup of warm milk or a snooze in the sunshine. I don't want enough of him to make me love a foreigner or pick beets with a migrant worker. I want ecstasy, not transformation; I want the warmth of a womb, not a new birth. I want a pound of the Eternal in a paper sack. I'd like to buy $3 worth of God, please.

WILBUR REES[1]

The Power of Discipleship

WHAT IF WE could tap into a place that brought ultimate fulfillment without all of life's ups and downs and abrupt changes? What if we could discover our God-given purpose in life and empower it with unabashed determination to achieve just that? What if we had a personal angel to point the way?

---

[1] Quoted in Joe E. Trull and James E. Carter, *Ministerial Ethics: Moral Formation for Church Leaders*, 2nd ed. (Grand Rapids: Baker Academic, 2004), 152–53.

I was about twelve years old when I gave my life to the Lord, was baptized, and attended Sunday school faithfully. My sisters and I were not required to go to church, so sometimes we chose to go, and other times we chose not to. During my college years, I attended less and less. About once a semester, an evangelistic minister would visit my campus. Students, myself included, would line up to get into the auditorium to hear his message, witness his charismatic ministry, and recommit our lives to the Lord. For several weeks following his visit, I was on a spiritual high. But over time, I would fall back into the same state as before his visit. In retrospect, I now realize that I had a see-saw relationship with God that lasted throughout my college life.

After graduating, I accepted a position as a development engineer with an aerospace company in Connecticut. I was born and raised in the south. The drastic change in climate, cultural norms, and communities, compared to my upbringing, took some getting used to. In my youth, my three sisters and I also experienced abrupt changes. We experienced military life while my dad was on active duty in the U.S. Air Force. We also lived with my grandmother on a farm in rural South Georgia for several years. We then transitioned from farm life to city life in a large urban community in central Florida and then to a more suburban community in north Florida with sidewalks, tennis courts, a golf course, and a community center.

My move to a small community in Connecticut was further challenged by not having any family or friends in the area. After about a year, I met a coworker from my hometown; we knew some of the same people, which was incredible. He was much older and quickly became like a father and a mentor to me. As he tells it, what he saw was a young woman whom he described as being book-smart and quick-witted but sheltered and somewhat naïve. He also saw this young woman as one who was spiritually lost but searching. Although he traveled to international locations regularly, he would always check on me when he was back in the U.S. He eventually led me to the Lord on one of his short stints at home. I share this story because when he led me to the Lord, it was different from all the previous times.

There was one profound factor that made all the difference that would transform my life. My newfound mentor talked about the importance of discipleship, a term of which I had very little understanding. He elaborated on the importance of connecting with others for prayer, Bible study, and fellowship. He didn't just talk about it. He took it upon himself to connect me with a woman who became to me like my personal angel. She prayed with me, taught me how to read the Bible, and, although she lived in a different city some distance away, she helped me connect to a church close to where I lived. I never met her in person; we talked only by telephone. I knew very little about her personal life, but in the short time that we communicated, I learned how to study the Bible and how to pray. Through prayer, I proliferated in my knowledge of, and in my relationship with, God. Though I don't have a clue regarding her appearance or family, she was a true example of a disciple of Christ. Because of the impact and influence she had in my life, I understand the power and significance of helping others—especially new converts—move beyond salvation, and into growing and sustaining their relationship with God. Discipleship is about helping others to grow in the Lord through transformation, teaching, praying, and doing. It is about setting an example for others to follow. It is a process that enables the new and growing believer to undergo a transformational process, and to find and pursue their God-given purpose in life.

From my own experience with discipleship, it is apparent to me that it is also about growth through a sacrificial response. A sacrificial response is making a biblically-based decision, regardless of how we feel or think. We are challenged every day to make choices that will either cause us to grow closer to God or will block our growth in God. The sacrificial response may be the path less chosen. It may be a lonelier journey, as many others follow the selective interpretations of the people and whatever is most popular. But, it is our sacrificial response that will enable and fuel our growth in God through transformation.

When we study the life of Jesus and how he called each of the twelve disciples to follow Him, we see it was not for the purpose of having supporters around Him to bolster his ministry. It wasn't to boost the numbers of his associates and followers. It was for one purpose: to make disciples of them, so that at an appropriate and appointed time, they would go forth and make disciples of others. During the ministry years of Christ, each disciple underwent a transformative process. Fleshly natures were revealed, as when Peter lashed out in anger and cut off the centurion's ear. Fears and doubts were exposed, as with doubting Thomas, who refused to believe that Christ had risen until he saw him in the flesh. The disciples' cultural influences and ideologies, which guided their thinking and way of life, challenged each of them to a new way of thinking. Each disciple faced his mirror for self-examination, experienced transformation, and ultimately realized God's plan.

A Self-Examination

There are numerous reports that provide estimates of the number of people professing to be Christians. Some reports also state that Christianity is among the fastest-growing religious groups. But how many of those professing to be Christian need transformation? The church today—like the church of the first century; a blend of people from many backgrounds, different traditions, and different belief systems—is challenged with setting a message capable of reaching Christians at many levels of growth, knowledge, and understanding of Biblical concepts. Additionally, some Christians may have become desensitized, and are merely going through the motions. I have had conversations with believers who have expressed fear of transformation.

There are preconceived notions about what transformation will do to them, or speculations about what must be given up. Sadly, some make deliberate decisions to avoid total submission and transformation, not realizing the blessings and prosperity that God has for us when we follow his plan.[2]

There exists a tremendous opportunity to experience the transforming work of the Holy Spirit, changing our nature into His likeness and image. However, a first step is illustrated in 2 Corinthians 13:5–8 which instructs us to examine ourselves:

> *Examine yourselves, to see whether you are in the faith. Test yourselves. Or do you not realize this about yourselves, that Jesus Christ is in you? —Unless indeed you fail to meet the test! I hope you will find out that we have not failed the test. But we pray to God that you may not do wrong—not that we may appear to have met the test, but that you may do what is right, though we may seem to have failed. For we cannot do anything against the truth, but only for the truth.*

Is there not enough finger-pointing, criticism, backbiting, idolatry, and judgment from other people? There are many discussions about wanting peace, not just in the world, but right in our own homes, in our communities, government, jobs and even in our churches. Some seek love from other people but have none to give. We want prosperity, but, as James 4:3 states, we ask and do not receive because we ask with the wrong motives. We ask with the purpose of fulfilling lustful desires.

What if we each faced the mirror to see for ourselves the internal attributes that are seen outwardly? What if we can better understand that not only can God transform us into His likeness and image, but by being transformed, we can also have a more profound impact in the

---

[2] Deuteronomy 29:9 Keep therefore the words of this covenant, and do them, that ye may prosper in all that ye do.

lives of others, because we exemplify a Christ-like nature? In Genesis 1:26, God said, "Let us make man in our image, after our likeness." What if this reflection had such a profound impact in the world that we could begin to see more peace, more love, and greater prosperity for all people? What if poverty and homelessness were non-existent because there was no greed? Are you ready for more significant transformation?

    I like the words of Mahatma Gandhi: "We must be the change we want to see in the world." I say change begins with us, and it must come from within.

A Personal Reflection

Mirror, Mirror:
What Reflection Do You See?

Questions for Thought and Reflection:

1. Have you experienced the power of discipleship in your life?

2. What are some of your internal attributes that are reflected outwardly and what do you think others see?

3. What does it mean to you to have $3 worth of God?

Chapter 2

The Mirror and Reflection!

Do not merely listen to the Word, and so deceive yourselves. Do what it says. Anyone who listens to the word but does not do what it says is like someone who looks at his face in a mirror and, after looking at himself, goes away and immediately forgets what he looks like.

—JAMES 1:22–24 (NIV)

What's in a Mirror?

IN THE RESEARCH and writing of this book, I have taken an interest in the history, origin, and use of the mirror. It appears that I am not alone. Mirrors have fueled people's intrigue and fascination for centuries. While we are most acquainted with the mirror as a looking glass, used to see a reflection of ourselves, its use is far-reaching. The mirror is used in many technological innovations, including the Hubble Space Telescope, modern solar ovens, and in power generators.[3]

An abundance of literature, both ancient and modern, discusses

---

[3] Mark Pendergrast, *Mirror Mirror: A History of the Human Love Affair with Reflection* (New York: Perseus, 2003), ix, x, 247.

reflections and various uses of the mirror. There are countless superstitions, myths, urban legends, and bits of folklore associated with the history of the mirror. Mirrors were among the most precious objects in ancient civilizations. Documented sources indicate that mirrors were used by the ancient Egyptians as early as 2900 BC.[4] The Old Testament also provides several illustrations of the use of bronze for mirrors. In a detailed account of Moses following the explicit instructions of Yahweh in constructing the Temple, Exodus 38:8 states, "He made the basin of bronze and its stand of bronze, from mirrors of the ministering women who ministered in the entrance of the tent of meeting". These were most likely mirrors brought from Egypt, commonly made from polished bronze. Job 37:18 also refers to a mirror constructed from cast bronze.

It is hard to imagine a life without mirrors, photographs, or images of some sort, but until around the thirteenth century, only the wealthy possessed looking-glasses, which were often just large enough to see their faces. Mirrors, as we know them today, remained a costly commodity during much of the sixteenth century and were considered a luxury, even among the wealthy. The mirror also experienced many transitions in production. Its earliest form was made from highly polished metals such as bronze or brass. It evolved to use silver-mercury amalgams and blown glass, which give us the clear, more accurate reflections that modern civilization is accustomed to.

Glass mirrors became essential to an aristocratic lady's toilette and were perhaps among her most prized possessions.[5] Women were loath to leave home without a mirror that fit comfortably in their purses. Mirrors were also considered to be a major commodity in household inventories during the eighteenth century.[6] As the mirror makers mea-

---

[4] Stephanie Lowder, "The History of Mirror: Through a Glass, Darkly," Bienenstock Furniture Library, at *http://www.furniturelibrary.com/mirror-glass-darkly/*.
[5] Ibid.
[6] Ibid.

surably improved their craft, the size of mirrors also increased from small, handheld objects to large, ornamental mirrors. It is perhaps difficult for us to imagine our own home without a single mirror, but we don't normally build our homes around our mirrors.

However, Louis XIV, King of France, did exactly that. He went to great extremes to create a wall of mirrors in the Palace of Versailles. This wall was known as the Grand Gallery, or, more commonly, the Hall of Mirrors. The Grand Gallery provided a full-length view, which was uncommon during that era. I remember my own experience of standing in sheer wonderment in the Hall of Mirrors. It was my favorite room in the palace. Its design and opulence were breathtaking. While this was a very costly project at that time, over time, as new and less-costly techniques of mirror production increased during the nineteenth century, mirrors became more familiar and accessible.

The Law of Reflection

Today, there are so many options to how mirrors can be used whether in home décor, grooming, or innovative technologies and devices. Mirrors seem to be everywhere. One can hardly escape wondering how to incorporate mirrors into the home décor. Scientist and technologists continue to discover innovative ways to advance useful purposes of the mirror. In this time, we are constantly observing ourselves or being observed.

While we can hardly escape the fascination with the mirror, it isn't per se about the mirror. It is something that extends far beyond its incredible aesthetic value. It is really all about the reflection. The mirror itself is only an instrument that is used to see a reflection of ourselves. These contraptions have also been the fuel for fantasy and vanity. Sadly, the mirror has been the cause of inflated egos and pride in some, while causing the demise of self-esteem and personal confidence in others.

While a main purpose of the mirror is to provide a reflection, do we always see that reflection, or do we see only what we want to see? When my daughters and I lived in Northern Virginia, we had a full-length mirror, which hung in the hallway on the third level of our townhouse. One weekend, while we were downstairs preparing a meal, we heard a loud crash from upstairs. For no apparent reason, that mirror had suddenly fallen off the wall and shattered. It was unexplainable, as it had safely hung there for at least five years. Without the mirror's presence, the hallway seemed dark and dull, and the wall looked bare. We quickly noticed the difference and decided to replace it. My younger daughter and I went shopping that very afternoon to find a new mirror.

As we shopped, my teenage daughter asked if she could inspect a prospective mirror I had chosen. I was quite curious about her level of expertise concerning mirrors, so I quickly accepted her suggestion, to see what she would do. She then asked me to steady the mirror in an upright position as she stepped a few feet away and then turned to check herself in the mirror. She quickly claimed that the mirror was not a good one and urged me to put it back. I was intrigued. But after she said the mirror made her appear too fat, I had an 'aha' moment! We went through this exercise several times more, as some made her seem too short or too skinny until we got one that she reasoned to be "just right." To her, the mirror had to provide a reflection that was to her liking and satisfaction. Never was there a thought that one of the rejected mirrors might have provided an accurate reflection.

How many of us, while window shopping, have taken note of our reflection in the storefront windows? Sometimes we may question what we see. *When did I gain all of that weight?* Or perhaps, *where did it come from? Can that reflection be accurate?* In the depths of our thoughts, we wonder how much distortion there is in the mirror. Are we looking for a "true" reflection or, do we want a mirror that gives us the reflection we want to see, while denying the truth?

The Mirror and Reflection!

I remember as a child going to the county fair. We were always excited about going and looked forward to that time of the year. There were so many attractions to choose from and, with limited funds, we had to choose carefully. One of my favorites was the House of Mirrors. There were all kinds of mirrors. Some made you look very tall and thin, with a body that curved in all sorts of ways. There were the mirrors that made you look short and fat, no matter how tall or skinny you were. The mirrors that I hated were the ones that magnified, showing every spot, pimple, wrinkle, and imperfection—because I had so many!

Many of us have things about ourselves that we don't like, so we go to extreme measures to avoid and pretend they don't exist. As a teenager, I wore heavy makeup because I didn't like the pimples. I worked hard at hiding all those imperfections. My classmates would laugh and taunt me. Some ridiculed me about the makeup while others teased me about my severe case of acne. No matter how much I tried to hide the pimples and fill in the oversized pores, they could still be seen.

Sometimes—perhaps more times than we will own up to—we see what we want to see and hear what we want to hear. We also see this in our Christian walk, where we justify and rationalize the Word of God to suit our lifestyles and behaviors. We may pray God's will, but when we face even the most minor decision, we choose what we want, according to the flesh. As the Scripture challenges us, are we one who may see our face in a mirror and, after seeing, go away and immediately forget what we look like? How quickly we forget our time with the Lord and the words we spoke in our prayers. How quickly we forget the sermon from our church services. If someone greeted us in the parking lot after the Sunday morning service, could we share a summary of that message? It can dissipate just that quickly.

Though mirrors are abundant and common in the marketplace today, much of their use is to observe the external. But what if we had mirrors that showed us our inner being? That is, a mirror that could see and reflect our nature, our character, and holiness? What if there were a mirror that could provide a rating of how we measure up inwardly compared to the image we show outwardly? What if?

Form and Substance

No matter how many tools exist in the marketplace today, sustained personal transformation is only possible by the workings of the Holy Spirit. We live in a society that places much emphasis on appearances, external beauty, fashion, and self-image. We are hard pressed to imagine not being able to see a reflection of ourselves daily. Vanity appears to have reached an all-time high with an abundant supply of makeover tools. Stores are filled with transformational options to help us with almost anything we want to do. There are manuals, books, and videos, for weight loss, body form, strength training, workouts, makeup, fashion, hair, and style.

There is also an emphasis on the external expression of internal traits. Our society emphasizes the ability to speak well and appear knowledgeable on a variety of subjects. Accordingly, there is an abundance of DIY tools to enhance our intellectual capacity, our knowledge, and our ability to communicate. There is an arsenal of material available to help us project self-esteem and confidence, and countless books about habits you should adopt or secrets you need to know and why you need to know them. The list is endless. Whatever you think you need or desire, there is a DIY manual or help available to you.

While the list of self-help material is endless, we often fail to achieve a sustainable transformation because we are attempting to recreate ourselves selectively and are more likely to miss the root cause. We also work from the outside, addressing those elements that are more appealing to others, because quite often, our motivations to change are driven by cultural and societal pressures to conform and fit in.

With the rising popularity of the DIY approach, we often attempt to transform ourselves spiritually. We mistakenly think that we are fully capable of achieving a sustainable transformation without allowing the Holy Spirit to work in us. Sustainable transformation is far different from achieving your goal. How many times have you heard or read stories about someone losing a considerable amount of weight only to regain it—and then some? Sometimes, we end up in a worse place than when we first began.

If it were possible for us to change our lives totally on our volition and will, it might be cause for us to boast and be prideful, thereby creating a wider separation from God.

Why then do we rely so heavily on the self-help propaganda? It appears that we are striving to improve ourselves and measure up to worldly standards. Are we caught up in a constant pursuit of the carnal things, or filled with puffed-up pride from worldly possessions, positions or perceived power (1 John 2:16)? As one of my favorite writers, Charles Finney, might ask, "What is the motive of the heart?" Are we seeking a true transformation that comes only from the work of the Holy Spirit?

Form is subjective. Form is generally seen as a person's external being, including facial features, figure and shape, curvature or muscularity. A well-known idiom says that "beauty is in the eye of the beholder." An appreciation of certain forms is guided by cultural and social norms. The media—television, radio, print, and social media—have a lot to say about what is beautiful, acceptable, or subpar defining what acceptable external attributes should look like. Some hypothesize that form without substance is shallow and nothing more than vanity.

The world is drawn to the external and is guided by form without consideration of one's internal makeup. But it is the internal that largely defines our true beauty and is the most substantive part of our being. As the saying goes, "beauty comes from within". Proverbs 31:30 tells us also that "beauty fades". As we grow older, our bodies change, showing obvious signs of aging. The youthful appearance that we had in high school or college becomes a thing of the past. Though we may exercise on a regular basis and eat nutritiously, our youthful features will change.

The good news is that aging brings wisdom, increased knowledge, and understanding. There are those who don't learn from life's experiences, but for those who do, age brings benefits. I think that age increases one's substance. Substance is the culmination of one's personality and intellectual capabilities, such as how smart they are, or how much education they have. It may be plain ol' common sense, or one's ability to manage life. In my life, I have seen positive change in many people around me as they age. I can also see how I have changed for the better. I can see an increase in my wisdom and discretion. I have a better temperament, am more giving and less selfish. I know that my patience is much better! Age, despite the fact that it is often denigrated for its physical effects, brings gifts in the areas that matter most.

As a teenager, one of my favorite commercials was a perfume commercial with a beautiful woman singing a song about herself. The lyrics went something like, "I can bring home the bacon, fry it up in a pan, and never let him forget he's a man; I'm a wo-man…" At the time, I thought that was symbolic of a woman with both beautiful form and incredible substance. Today, I look to many Biblical examples of great women with excellent form and generous substance. Some of my favorites are Queen Esther, Naomi, the unnamed woman of Proverbs 31, the Persistent Widow, and Mother Mary. Each of these beautiful and phenomenal women experienced transformation, overcame suffering, and sorrow. They were victorious in overcoming some life challenge that was beyond their human capacity to ultimately accomplish God's purpose and plan.

While we each may have our view of desired attributes, scripture tells us that we are *"fearfully and wonderfully made"* (Psalm 139:14). Peter makes it clear that, *"Your beauty should not come from outward adornment, such as elaborate hairstyles and the wearing of gold jewelry or fine clothes. Rather, it should be that of your inner self, the unfading beauty of a gentle and quiet spirit, which is of great worth in God's sight (1 Peter 3:3-4 NIV).*

Transformation is a place of total surrender. We reach this place when we realize that whatever we are grappling with may be beyond our human capacity. Transformation is also about trusting in God to lead and guide us through his agenda. He has more for us than what we realize or can even comprehend. It is comforting and reassuring to know that when we put our trust in God, we can have complete victory. *"The blessing of the LORD makes rich, and he adds no sorrow with it"* (Proverbs 10:22).

A Misaligned Confession

We must be truthful with ourselves. The confession of our faith must match up with our character and behaviors, as in Hebrews 10:23, "Let us hold fast the confession of our hope without wavering, for he who promised is faithful." A spiritual transformation is possible only by the work of the Holy Spirit, which requires our participation through commitment and obedience. Any other approach is hypocritical. Attempts to possess the things of God while circumventing the transformational process is what some refer to as a 'back-door' approach. It is descriptive of those who embrace God's blessings but have hearts that are far from God and resort to doing things their way. As we face the mirror, there must be a realization that God has instituted a divine order and transparency in our relationship with Him. It must not be dishonored by pretense or hypocrisy.

Those who claim to be Christian must endeavor to safeguard Christianity's integrity, unity, and purity by setting forth a reflection of Christ Jesus. It is a work that must begin on the inside. When the soul or inner being sincerely desires more of God, then change will take place. Without even working at it, you will begin to love your neighbor, have compassion for that coworker whom you have in the past only criticized, or begin to see the severe challenges which plagued you in the past start to melt away. It is about soul transformation. You can change your behaviors, but only God can change your heart.

Can you think of an example of how we can truly exemplify the character and nature of Christ? Can you think of an example of someone attempting to do so, but ultimately revealing a disingenuous and hypocritical nature?

The Truth Be Known

After the death, resurrection, and ascension of Christ, the disciples remained in Jerusalem and, as promised, received the power and anointing of the Holy Spirit. The book of Acts describes how they immediately set out on a mission in a response to the call of the "great commission". The great commission that Christ commands of his disciples is to go into all the world and share his good news. This great commission is a charge for all of Christ's disciples, even today. It entails far more than preaching. It includes exercising great compassion and concern for the poor, the fatherless, the widowed, and for one another. The people described in the Book of Acts moved beyond obsession with ownership of earthly possessions and gave generously and freely. "There was not a needy person among them, for as many as were owners of lands or houses sold them and brought the proceeds of what was sold and laid it at the apostles' feet, and it was distributed to each as any had need" (Acts 4:34–35).

Among them was a Levite named Joseph but called Barnabas (which means "son of encouragement"), who "sold a field that belonged to him and brought the money [from the sale] and laid it at the apostles' feet" (v. 37). Barnabas was known as a man with a good heart and was trustworthy. With zeal, he sold his property and gave so that others in need could have. Ananias and his wife Sapphira also sold land that they owned. Some might presume that Ananias and Sapphira observed what Barnabas had done and, perhaps seeing the recognition and tribute given to Barnabas for his actions, set out to do the same, or even to outdo Barnabas. The text states:

> *"A man named Ananias, with his wife Sapphira sold a piece of property, and with his wife's knowledge he kept back for himself some of the proceeds and brought only a part of it and laid it at the apostles' feet. But Peter said, "Ananias, why has Satan filled your heart to lie to the Holy Spirit and to keep back for yourself part of the proceeds of the land? While it remained unsold, did it not remain your own? And after it was sold, was it not at your disposal? Why is it that you have contrived this deed in your heart? You have not lied to man but to God." When Ananias heard these words, he fell down and breathed his last. And great fear came upon all who heard of it. The young men rose and wrapped him up and carried him out and buried him.*
>
> *After about three hours his wife came in, not knowing what had happened. And Peter said to her, "Tell me whether you sold the land for so much." And she said, "Yes, for so much." But Peter said to her, "How is it that you have agreed together to test the Spirit of the Lord? Behold, the feet of those who have buried your husband are at the door, and they will carry you out." Immediately she fell down at his feet and breathed her last. When the young men came in, they found her dead, and they carried her out and buried her beside her husband. And great fear came upon the whole church and upon all who heard of these things (Acts 5:1–11)."*

Ananias' property was his to do with as he pleased, both before it was sold and after. He was under no obligation to sell it or donate any amount of the funds from the proceeds. Nor was there any obligation or pressure to give it away, in part or whole. It was Ananias who schemed to give a portion of the proceeds while making it appear that he was giving all the proceeds to the Church. The Holy Spirit revealed the deception and the motives of his heart to Peter. Ananias' sin was not to the people; it was a sin unto God. Did Ananias think that God did not see or know what he had done? Doesn't God know the motives of our hearts and hear our impure thoughts? Was Ananias trying to project an image of himself that was, in reality, quite different? Was he attempting to be seen doing a great deed before the apostles and the people, to receive praise and notoriety? Was the true reflection cast by Ananias and Sapphira an impure motive, driven by a narcissistic nature? Some have questioned if it was a 'sin unto death'. What factors led to the demise of Ananias and Sapphira? While there are many theological perspectives and commentaries concerning this account, there is one view, from an unknown writer, that offers a credible hermeneutical viewpoint. The author indicates that "the impact of Ananias' and Sapphira's actions had little or nothing to do with greed or self-interest, but everything to do with being a false witness. The consequence of their planned scheme cost them their lives, not because they lied to the apostles, or the people. The consequence and impact of their deception could have had the most extreme effect on the developing Church and the unbelieving world. Their seemingly-insignificant deception misrepresented Christ and His gospel to those who were watching." Some suggest it was a response to protect the advancement of the church's formation and to guard against the proliferation of such seductive inducements. "Every way of a man is right in his own eyes, but the Lord weighs the heart" (Proverbs 21:2).

Vanity of Vanities

We are influenced by the world every day. When we look in the mirror, we perhaps have some, if not many, thoughts about what we see, while determining how close we measure up to those worldly influences and artificial metrics. The Lord sent the prophet Samuel to the home of Jesse to anoint one of his sons to become the next king of Israel. Samuel was not given a name, photo, or vision of what the new king looked like but was merely instructed to go and anoint one of Jesse's sons. Jesse immediately brought his oldest son, David's oldest brother, before Samuel. As Samuel looked upon Jesse's first born, he heard the voice of the Lord, just as he'd heard the voice of the Lord as a young lad: "Do not look on his appearance or the height of his stature, because I have rejected him. For the LORD sees not as man sees: man looks on the outward appearance, but the LORD looks on the heart" (1 Samuel 16:7).

God sees our true reflection, no matter what fine-looking mirror we stand in front of. The book of Ecclesiastes also counsels us that "all is vanity." The Hebrew word translated as "vain" is אוש, pronounced "sheva," and means "empty, or having no meaning, insincere." It also means "false," as in the Mosaic commandment, "Thou shalt not take the LORD's name falsely" or "Thou shalt not speak or act in the name or character of Elohim falsely." In other words, don't say you're a Christian and then act in a manner that does not reflect who God is.[7]

While the book of Ecclesiastes exposes truths about the meaning of life; it affirms that the meaning of life is not about what the world has to offer but is about the Creator of all life. Ecclesiastes describes vanity as a life filled with striving after pleasure; obsessed with things that satisfy the flesh: seeking self-recognition, human knowledge, or philosophies, for personal gain. King Solomon, who also wrote the book of Ecclesiastes, further describes vanity as a drive for fame, popularity,

---

7 *http://deborahsexton.hubpages.com/hub/TheMisunderstanding-Of-Biblical-Hebrew-Words-The-True- Definitions*, site accessed August 2016.

and wealth, constantly seeking first and foremost to fulfill the desires of the flesh and selfish ambitions.

Mark the Evangelist asks, "For what does it profit a man to gain the whole world and forfeit his soul" (Mark 8:36)? It sends a strong message that we can deceive ourselves and could be eternally lost if we pursue worldly goods, possessions, or the pleasures of life to the detriment of spiritual pursuits. Solomon had everything the world could offer and yet, in the end, he declares that there is nothing or anyone greater than God. He provides wise counsel regarding the conclusion of the whole matter, and that is to, "Fear God and keep his commandments, for this is the whole duty of man. For God will bring every deed into judgment, with every secret thing, whether good or evil" (Ecclesiastes 12:13–14). The Apostle John provides counsel in 1 John 2:15-17. He states, "Do not love the world or the things in the world. If anyone loves the world, the love of the Father is not in him. For all that is in the world—the desires of the flesh and the desires of the eyes and the pride in possessions—is not from the Father but is from the world. And the world is passing away along with its desires, but whoever does the will of God abides forever".

Moving Beyond the External

Church pews are filled with people who have religious 'convictions' and yet live as they choose, unaligned with biblical teachings. They have one foot in the church and the other planted in the world. It is a hypocritical projection. While their words indicate that they are Christian, the inner reflection falls short. They have no real zeal for God. They might also hold an image in their minds of what they think they look like, no matter what the mirror projects. They may rationalize that the mirror is defective, and not actually casting a true reflection, but in reality, they often refuse to let go of the image they believe that they see.

If we focus only on the external properties of reflection, we lose sight of the centrality of this message: the inward nature reflected outwardly. Genesis 1:27 says that during the time of creation, God created male and female in His image. There has been continual debate about the exact meaning of this Scripture. Humankind through the centuries has attempted to discover who God is and get a glimpse of his appearance. Moses asked to get just a glimpse of this great and powerful supernatural being who burned in a bush yet did not consume the bush. Moses asks to see God. Exodus 33:19–23 recounts the Lord's reply: And he said,

> *"I will make all my goodness pass before you and will proclaim before you my name 'The LORD.' And I will be gracious to whom I will be gracious and will show mercy on whom I will show mercy. But," he said, "You cannot see my face, for man shall not see me and live." And the LORD said, "Behold, there is a place by me where you shall stand on the rock, and while my glory passes by I will put you in a cleft of the rock, and I will cover you with my hand until I have passed by. Then I will take away my hand, and you shall see my back, but my face shall not be seen."*

Moses was permitted to see the Lord only as He passed by and not permitted to have a direct look at His face. There is something about the face of God—a radiance and magnificence, a glow that is beyond description—that to look upon it would perhaps be too much for human beings to handle in our present bodily form. I can recall many times in my childhood years, along with other playmates, attempting to figure out the sun, foolishly staring directly into it. Our human capacity to do so was substantially limited. We could not even advance to the stage of "staring." We could only get a quick look for a second or two before our eyes would either tear up or experience temporary blindness and dizziness. I imagine that the face of God must be as radiant as the sun. It is certainly too much for our human forms to look upon. There are many writings and discussions about how we are made in the image and likeness of God. Many have focused on the exterior, or the physical attributes, rather than our internal or spiritual attributes. If we are made in the image and likeness of God, our Creator, what exactly does that mean? The word 'image' occurs 147 times in the King James Bible, with 124 occurrences in the Hebrew context. The Hebrew word צֶלֶם, and its transliteration *tselem*, pronounced "tseh'·lem," is from an unused root, meaning 'to shade' or 'a phantom', i.e., (figuratively) illusion, resemblance; hence, a representative figure.[8]

While we are made in the image and likeness of God, we are born with a sinful nature because of the fall of man in the Garden of Eden. Romans 5:12 indicates that "sin came into the world through one man, and death through sin, and so death spread to all men because all sinned." However, God made provision to redeem humankind and to restore us to a relationship with Him. God sent his son, Jesus, to free us from the power of sin. Through His death and resurrection, we can be reconciled with God. "Therefore, as one trespass led to condemnation for all men, so one act of righteousness leads to justification and life for all men. For as by the one man's disobedience the many were made sinners, so by the one man's obedience the many will be made righteous" (Romans 5:18–19). Reconciliation is available to all through salvation—a gift that must be accepted.

God Sheds Light Through Others

One aspect of mirrors that we haven't discussed, but is essential in understanding how they work, is that mirrors work only in the presence of light. Most objects, that have a smooth surface and reflect light,

---

[8] James Strong, *The New Strong's Exhaustive Concordance of the Bible* (Nashville: Thomas Nelson, 2001).

can be a mirror. There are over one hundred verses in the Bible about 'light.' A few of my favorites are:

"In the same way, let your light shine before others, so that they may see your good works and give glory to your Father who is in heaven" (Matthew 5:16).

"You are the light of the world. A city set on a hill cannot be hidden" (Matthew 5:14).

"Your word is a lamp to my feet and a light to my path" (Psalm 119:105).

"Then shall your light break forth like the dawn, and your healing shall spring up speedily; your righteousness shall go before you; the glory of the Lord shall be your rear guard" (Isaiah 58:8).

While there are so many others, a recurring theme is that the Holy Spirit and the Scriptures provide light. As disciples of Christ, we are called to be guiding lights for others, either by example or by correction. There are many biblical accounts of times when the prophets were sent to shine light, but the people did not receive them. The prophets were often scorned, ridiculed, beheaded, or crucified. But it is possible to become desensitized to sin to the point of ignoring or not recognizing the warnings. Our conscience may speak conviction, but will we stop and pay attention, or choose to ignore the warning signs that ring aloud like sirens. We can easily rationalize and justify our desires, convincing ourselves that our actions and motives are pure and acceptable. It is God's word that provides truth and the light. It is our conscience and guide to all matters of life.

Because God sees the heart condition of man, in His infinite mercy and grace, sends His prophets or messengers to shine light, bring correction, or simply be an example of Christ Jesus. Sometimes, people show up in our lives and appear seemingly out of nowhere and bring the comfort, help, and support we need. It is as though the Angels have appeared in human form to be our advocate and deliverers. There are also times when people seem to show up in our lives and bring conflict. While it may be difficult for us to tolerate such behavior or to walk in the light and love of Christ, through patience and prayer, we can be victorious. But the more we disregard biblical approaches and point a finger, the more we deny the transformative work of the Holy Spirit.

An example of how God uses others to help us see our indiscretions, let's look at 2 Samuel 12: 1-6, recording a God-ordained encounter between the prophet Nathan and King David:

> *"And the LORD sent Nathan to David." He came to him and said to him, "There were two men in a certain city, the one rich and the other poor. The rich man had very many flocks and herds, but the poor man had nothing but one little ewe lamb, which he had bought. And he brought it up, and it grew up with him and with his children. It used to eat of his morsel and drink from his cup and lie in his arms, and it was like a daughter to him. Now there came a traveler to the rich man, and he was unwilling to take one of his own flock or herd to prepare for the guest who had come to him, but he took the poor man's lamb and prepared it for the man who had come to him." Then David's anger was greatly kindled against the man, and he said to Nathan, "As the LORD lives, the man who has done this deserves to die, and he shall restore the lamb fourfold, because he did this thing, and because he had no pity."*

David not only received Nathan the prophet and listened. He was also incensed with the account of how a rich man with so much could take all that belonged to the poor man, which was so little, and leave him with nothing. David even pronounced the judgment that should come upon the person. Like David, we sometimes find it easy to deflect our own sin and pronounce judgment on others. It is easy to point the finger at another when we think our hands are clean and without guilt. At the point he passed judgement, David had not yet recognized the sin that he committed or the error of his ways in taking another man's wife—his *only* wife. David had many wives and concubines. Yet he misused his authority to steal another man's and then killed that man to conceal it. Arranging for Uriah to be killed in battle was no different than drawing the sword himself.

There are some who think that if they can seduce someone else to do the "dirty work," their hands are left clean. For example, someone who deliberately attempts to destroy a person's reputation by dropping "gossip bombs" to a person they know will spread it like wildfire, is not guiltless. People in places of high authority can't command others to carry out their revenge or use their position to get even or bring harm to others because of personal feelings or vendettas and remain sinless. The prophet Nathan made clear to David that he was accountable for the transgressions that were committed against Uriah and Bathsheba. The prophet spoke openly and boldly that David was the offender. Nathan said to David,

> *"You are the man! Thus says the LORD, the God of Israel, 'I anointed you king over Israel, and I delivered you out of the hand of Saul. And I gave you your master's house and your master's wives into your arms and gave you the house of Israel and Judah. And if this were too little, I would add to you as much more. Why have you despised the word of the LORD, to do what is evil in his sight? You have struck down Uriah the Hittite with the sword and have taken his wife to be your wife and have killed him with the sword of the Ammonites.'" (2 Samuel: 7–9)*

David's sin harmed not only his neighbor but also impacted his own family. This biblical passage shows that God made David aware of his sin. It was God who blessed him and chose him to be king, elevating him to a place of high stature and responsibility. All that David possessed was a result of God's divine presence in David's life who made all these things possible. The Lord even told David that if this had not been enough, He would have added more. We are accountable to God. We are not to take matters into our own hands, but trust that the Lord provides all of our needs. When we delight ourselves in Him, He gives us the desires of our heart (Psalm 37:4).

The Mirror and Reflection!

Mirror, Mirror:
What Reflection Do You See?

Questions for Thought and Reflection!

1. Can you describe an occasion where your motives for doing something were vastly different from what you portrayed?

2. Can you identify emotions in your heart that have not been dealt with?

Chapter 3

Your Slip Is Hanging!

I RECALL, AS A young girl, hearing some of the older ladies of the church talking among themselves, making comments about a woman's slip hanging. They questioned one another, asking, "Did you see her slip hanging? It was hanging a mile long. Somebody should take her aside and help her." I recall thinking that I knew the person they made comments about and did not observe her slip hanging. Though I was very young at the time, it didn't take me too long to conclude that they weren't talking about her physical slip or underskirt. It became apparent to me that the 'slip hanging' was a code that there was something wrong in this woman's personal life. Like a slip, whatever was showing was not supposed to show. It was meant to be hidden and concealed, but obviously wasn't so neatly tucked away. Although the woman thought she had it all together, her life was really all hanging out and exposed. Whatever she had done Saturday night had made it to church before she did on Sunday morning, and everybody knew it—except her.

This example does not only apply to women. Men also attempt to conceal their indiscretions, with as little success. The bottom line is that secrets don't remain secrets forever. Whatever is hidden comes to light.

The media has exposed many highly visible and notable individuals for varying indiscretions. We have seen or heard shocking news of well-known church leaders, politicians, and community leaders held in the highest regard—even among our nation's presidents. However, the purpose of this book is not to name names and point fingers, but to set the image of Christ—his nature and character—that we are called to reflect. We should face the mirror and see a complete reflection of ourselves. We have much about ourselves to be concerned with, rather than looking at someone else's clutter. No one is perfect. Therefore, no one can justifiably point the finger at someone else's indiscretions. To do so, subjects them to scrutiny.

Here again, this book is not about putting anyone on display, but to illustrate behaviors. I recall an example of a high-profile leader where the media bombarded the airways with news of an improper relationship with a young woman. I was appalled that many indulged themselves in the salacious details of what reportedly transpired. Many people pointed fingers and hurled accusations, but then the lights of the media began to turn from the accused to the accusers. Those who had cast judgment and proposed punishment quickly scurried to flee the light, because, the media reported, they also had their personal indiscretions.

Sometimes we carry the guilt of unconfessed sin. It becomes sin compounded on top of sin or unforgiveness that has also compounded. Those who do evil hate the light because they fear that their conduct will be exposed (John 3:20). There are emotions we may not understand, and some are deep within. We attempt to put forth the best appearance that we can on the outside, with designer clothes, or personal or professional accomplishments. Inside, we are filled with shame, disappointment, bitterness, unforgiveness, or compounded anger over past mistakes or experiences. While we all have sinned, there are some who attempt to conceal their sins. If habitual, that person may then resort to diverse antics to cover up their sin. However, it usually doesn't end there. They may then lie to cover-up the sin and then cover-up the cover-up. Over time, that person may have trouble remembering which version of the story was told to which person until that behavior is completely exposed. There are some who try to run, hide, or pretend something didn't happen or doesn't exist. But whatever "it" is, it can never be hidden from God, who is omnipotent, omniscient, and omnipresent. You may ask, who is it that we should confess to? Confession of sin is always to God. There are times when we may need to confess to someone and ask forgiveness if we have wronged someone. If you lust after a person secretly in your heart, then that confession is made to God. But, if you act on your lustful thoughts toward a person and you have inappropriate behavior with that person, then you need to confess your wrong with that person and ask forgiveness from that person and God.

Certain behaviors can go on for years to the point where we not only think that it must be acceptable, but it also becomes a way of life and a part of our nature. It can change our behavior, our outlook on life, and our interactions with other people. There is a great value in those who are cognizant enough to recognize that there is a cover-up and a need for God to do a transformational work.

Freedom in Confession

Through my personal experience as a confidante, and life coach, I have observed that there are some who would rather take their secrets to the grave rather than confess them. Holding on to secret things are like vices that grip and stagnate our lives. There is also more pressure and stress associated with trying to keep things a secret than openly confessing them and being set free. The biblical reference to being set free does not only pertain to the issue that besets you, but also to being set free from the bondage and weight of a sinful nature. It is being set free from carrying the weight and burden of past entanglements and indiscretions, knowing that we are righteous again before the Father. It is being set free from the sinful nature that unknowingly attached itself to us, causing us to desire unnatural things or to veer in a direction contrary to the pathway that God has created just for us. It is being set free from ideological and intellectual bantering, causing us to miss or dismiss what God is telling us through His Word, the Scriptures. Being set free enables us to do and be all that God has granted us and to fulfill His purpose for our lives. It enables us to experience the fullness of God's peace and joy in our lives and thereby, bring peace and joy in our relationships and encounters with others. When we are beset by heaviness, it will eventually manifest itself outwardly.

People fear confession for a plethora of reasons. Some people fear confession because of the consequences they think they may suffer. Some fear that their reputation or image will be tarnished. No matter the reason, it is a biblical mandate. Scripture tells us that when we confess our sins to God and our hearts are humbled, then God will remember his covenant with us (Leviticus 26:40). Proverbs 28:13 tells us that "Whoever conceals his transgressions will not prosper, but he who confesses and forsakes them will obtain mercy." In Psalm 32:1, David declares, "Blessed is the one whose transgression is forgiven, whose sin in covered. Blessed is the man against whom the Lord counts no iniquity, and in whose spirit, there is no deceit." David goes on to describe how his bones wasted away and a heaviness was upon him when he kept silent concerning his iniquities. When we confess our sin, the Lord is just to forgive us and restore us in the right relationship.

A Covering versus a Cover-Up

Whether we attempt to cover-up things done out of shame and embarrassment or just refuse to face the truth, we must recognize the difference in "a covering" and a "cover-up." There are some who try to cover-up their indiscretions or indiscretions of others to protect their friends or their own image. Regardless, we must understand the difference. A cover-up is simply an effort to protect or conceal the truth—for example, the truth about one's self, another person, or a situation. It is when we know something and refuse to share or confess what we know.

Having worked in a university setting in recent years, I observed that there were many times when students would cover-up for their friends, roommates, or campus cohort who may be involved with multiple partners. I can recall engaging in some of those actions from my own college days. Sometimes, we don't want to expose another because we don't want to reveal our friends or ourselves. That old aphorism "birds of a feather flock together" has some truth to it. We were smart enough in college to at least consider that if others knew the real character of our friend, they would perhaps think that we were no different. So, there were probably more cover-ups were going on than we knew about.

At times, we may cover up not only the acts of others but also matters concerning ourselves. Jesus knew that Peter would publicly deny that he was one of His disciples. He warned Peter that he would betray Him three times before the cock crowed twice. Mark 14:72 provides an account of Peter's denial, "And the second time the cock crew ... Peter called to mind the word that Jesus said unto him, Before the cock crow twice, thou shalt deny me thrice" (KJV). When the woman recognized Peter as one of those with Jesus, Peter attempted to cover up and deny his association with Jesus.

We have seen this same behavior in our time. Some people surround themselves with great leaders—those in powerful positions of influence, stature, and visibility. When the great leader is discovered to have committed some indiscretion and faces public humiliation, the followers quickly fall away. They, like Peter, disassociate themselves, adopting a disingenuous, I–never-knew-the-person posture. It is as though the relationship never existed.

There are those who attempt to cover-up for others or themselves to hide ungodly behaviors or character flaws, and resort to extreme measures to keep their secrets hidden. Do they not understand that we serve an all-knowing God? Yet, they deliberately shield their actions and keep them secret for as long as they can. One can only imagine the number of secrets that people have taken with them to the grave. The grip was so tight such that truth would never be revealed. Through the years, I have seemingly attracted people who sought a confidant. I have come to recognize it as a gift from God and perhaps the beginning steps of discipleship by me and transformation for them. As previously mentioned, there have been conversations where the individual defiantly declared that they would rather take some secrets to the grave rather than openly confess them. Again, the things done in secret are not hidden from God. He is all-knowing and omniscient. He is also a forgiving God.

Sometimes we know those areas that we need to face and own. We may recognize that we have an anger management issue or a problem with pornography or secret desires. We may realize that we do not forgive others and will hold a grudge and seek to get even or secretly hope for the failure of other people we dislike. While the list of issues can go on and on, the question is, can you face the mirror?

Slip Hanging and Exposed

Exposure can be intentional or unintentional. It can come from oneself or others. What we are talking about here is exposing the inner being. It's about the woman with her slip hanging or the man who lost his game. It is about showing who we are: our character, our nature, our behaviors, or more pointedly, our true colors. Let's look at both—unintentional exposure and intentional exposure—and dig deeper into their meaning and significance.

Your Slip Is Hanging!

Someone asked a specific question concerning this topic: if your slip is hanging—meaning all your business is exposed—don't you feel the draft? A friend shared an experience with me that I think is a good illustration of what can happen in an accidental or unintentional exposure. She was recently at a restaurant and observed a woman's garments all askew as she came out of the ladies' room. Her dress was clinging to her underwear and was not completely pulled down over her hips, leaving one side of her undergarment exposed. On top of that, she had a glob of toilet paper hanging onto the heel of her shoe and trailing behind her. My friend noticed people in the restaurant pointing, whispering, and snickering at the woman, but no one offered to inform her or help. My friend approached the woman and gently escorted her back into the ladies' room to show her the problem and help correct the matter.

Jesus encountered a woman who had a major indiscretion exposed, one that was intentional and could have resulted in her death, based on the cultural norms of that period. How did he handle it?

The Gospel of John tells of a woman brought by many men before Jesus, shouting and declaring her to be an adulterous woman. John's account says that the scribes and the Pharisees brought a woman who had been caught in adultery, and placing her in the midst they said to Him,

> *"Teacher, this woman has been caught in the act of adultery. Now in the Law, Moses commanded us to stone such women. So, what do you say?" This they said to test him that they might have some charge to bring against him. Jesus bent down and wrote with his finger on the ground. And as they continued to ask him, he stood up and said to them, "Let him who is without sin among you be the first to throw a stone at her." And once more he bent down and wrote on the ground. But when they heard it, they went away one by one, beginning with the older ones, and Jesus was left alone with the woman standing before him. Jesus stood up and said to*

her, "Woman, where are they? Has no one condemned you?" She said, "No one, Lord." And Jesus said, "Neither do I condemn you; go, and from now on sin no more." (John 8:3–11)

Shamelessly, and with great excitement, the accusers who had brought the woman had already condemned her. Not only were they anxious to expose her exploits and publicly humiliate her, but they were equally as anxious to stone her. But where was the other participant in the adultery? Why was his sin covered up, while the woman was not only exposed, but set up to pay the price with her life? Yes, she was guilty, but a person's reaction to seeing another person exposed is just as revealing as the exposure of the sin itself. What will you do when you see someone exposed? Will we stand by, whisper, and ridicule, like the bystanders in the restaurant? Or will we stand ready to humiliate, disgrace, and condemn, like those in the Gospel account?

Jesus's response was one of shining light on those who stood ready to stone another, thinking themselves so pious. His response, "Let he who is without sin cast the first stone," was a challenge that required an immediate self-assessment. They had no choice at that moment but to face the mirror. With an honest assessment, those who stood ready to condemn could not act, and began to dismiss themselves. You can probably imagine them doing some smooth back steps, just quietly moonwalking backwards and completely out of the picture, trying not to be noticed.

The woman who stood exposed before Jesus was not only set free from those who stood ready to condemn her; she was also instructed by a merciful Jesus to go and live a life free from sin. When our sin is forgiven, we are reproved to go and sin no more. We receive grace, mercy, and forgiveness from God. He covers our sin so completely and thoroughly that it is never remembered again. Like the adulterous woman, He also calls us to live a different way, a transformed way.

Have you ever experienced when someone who has known you from childhood remembers everything about you and continually brings it up? In conversations, this person will go back to things you may have forgotten and try to paint a picture of you like your old self. Although you have forgiven, been forgiven, forgotten, and moved on, this childhood friend wants to keep reminding you repeatedly. Thankfully, we serve a God who is full of grace and mercy. He cast our sins away from us as far as the east is from the west and they are not remembered (Isaiah 43:25 and Psalms 103.12).

Each time I read the story about the adulteress, I ponder what happened to the woman's partner? I have also had discussions with theologians and other biblical scholars and there are many speculations. Perhaps you have also wondered about the woman's partner and why he is so blatantly absent from the story. Old Testament scripture indicates that in cases of adultery, both the man and the woman are to be stoned. However, the story does not indicate that the woman's partner was brought forth and exposed. Was he deliberately shielded, or did he manage to escape? Perhaps we could even hypothesize that his indiscretions were deliberately covered up by the same men who brought the woman. From Biblical accounts, the woman was repentant and received forgiveness, deliverance and freedom when she encountered Jesus. It is likely that her partner did not learn the error of his ways and therefore, maintained a propensity for adultery. While the woman was subjected to public humiliation for her sin, God desires that we confess our sin and repent as soon as we commit that sin. We can attempt to run and hide until it catches up with us in an unlikely situation which could include public exposure as we have seen in media accounts.

The book of James tells us to, confess our sins to one another and pray for one another, that we may be healed. This also includes healing and deliverance from sins of the flesh. While we are to be transparent, there is also an element of discretion in who we confess our sins to.

That person must be someone who has spiritual maturity to pray with you and for you. The latter part of the scripture says that the prayer of a righteous person has great power and produces great results (James 5:16). There are people who have impure hearts and vindictive motives who would take your sincere confessions and attempt to humiliate you or destroy your reputation. Confession of our sin is an acknowledgement that we see ourselves. It is an opportunity for God to do a transformative work and ultimately equip us to be effective examples and disciples for his work. God holds the plan and vision for our life, but we undergo a process of transformation like being fine-tuned on the potter's wheel. Jeremiah assures us that God knows the plans he has for us and they are good plans to prosper us not harm or disaster and plans to give us a future and hope (Jeremiah 29:11).

Another great example found in the Gospel of John, while walking through Samaria, Jesus encounters another woman, drawing water from a well. She thought she was only getting water at a well, as usual, but there she meets Jesus. Jesus exposes her life by telling her all about herself: "Go, call your husband, and come here." The woman answered him, "I have no husband." Jesus said to her, "You are right in saying, 'I have no husband'; for you have had five husbands, and the one you now have is not your husband. What you have said is true" (John 4:16–18). Perhaps she, too, was the subject of many conversations within the town. Maybe people criticized her for her lack of moral character. I wonder if anyone in the town ever constructively approached her. Either this was not the case, or she refused wise counsel until Jesus entered her life. It was her encounter with Jesus at the well and confession of her sinful ways that brought about change. There was no public humiliation. There was only confession, forgiveness and transformation. While Christ transformed the woman at the well, it is the work of the Holy Spirit that transforms us and prepares us for greater discipleship. However, we must be willing participants to allow the work of the Holy

Spirit to take place. Sometimes, we resist and ultimately find ourselves in situations that brings us to a place of submission and transformation as we have seen in the biblical illustrations in this section.

Exposure Requires a Response

That brings me to my closing point and that is, there is a response required when we are exposed. The adulterous woman received mercy and forgiveness and was set free from being stoned but moreover, set free from the destructive vices of sin. Likewise, the woman at the well repented and received forgiveness. In both cases, the women were instructed to go and sin no more. But what about the accusers, observers and bystanders? Maybe we are not the one who is exposed. Sometimes our casual observation may be the way that God will have us face the mirror. We may see something in another person that uncovers something in our life. It may be a lack of compassion. Maybe we are quick to judge and condemn others. While God is merciful and just to forgive us of our sin and unrighteousness, we may find it difficult to forgive others and hold onto anger and bitterness for years. We may see a behavior in someone else, but we refuse to acknowledge that we have areas in need of transformation.

What has been our response to observing others' situations? Our response can be an indication of our inner nature. I recall watching the movie Hotel Rwanda, based on a true story about the brave acts of a hotelier to save the lives of his family and more than a thousand other refugees by granting them shelter in a besieged four-star hotel during the 1994 Rwandan genocide. While the movie exposed genocide, political corruption, and the repercussions of violence, there is one scene where the hotelier argued with a foreign news reporter. He desired for the news reporter to arouse the nations to come to their defense by sending the news across the world. The reporter responded by saying,

"The people will see and say, 'Oh my God, that's horrible,' and go on eating their dinner."

What is our response to matters we observe? Do we show a lack of compassion or concern? Are we quick to cast blame, point a finger, gossip, laugh, ridicule, or demean others for their situations? Do we pretend to be a good friend, trusted coworker, or caring family member, but have ulterior motives? Rather than displaying kindness, patience, compassion, or other Christ-like attributes, do we allow the flesh to rule?

Sometimes, there may be situations like the Rwandan genocide, where we may think that there is little that we can do that might have an impact. While activism can make a difference, be it contacting your elected official, writing an Op-ed, or providing financial support, there is one response that we can make that is all powerful and transcends in geographical, physical and political realms, and that is prayer. It is one action not to be taken lightly though so many seem to put it last on the list of things to do. We would do ourselves and others a disservice to underestimate the power of fasting and prayer. It is the effectual fervent prayers of the righteous that profits significantly (James 5:16). Even in situations that we may encounter in our daily lives, we can and should be covering others, knowing that we too may be subjected to circumstances beyond our ability to manage. It's not a cover-up but a covering; a covering in prayer should be our first response.

I have established many teleconferenced prayer calls over the past decade. Many of these prayer groups still exist today. Participants come and go but the prayer calls continue. We have seen members of some calls here in the U.S. return to their native homelands and start new prayer calls there. The salient point about the prayer calls is the impact. We have seen many, many prayers answered. Situations have been miraculously turned around. People suddenly found jobs after looking for many months. Relationships have been mended. In addition to families and situations close to us, we have experienced answers to many prayers for people we hardly knew or know only through news reports about situations around the globe. We have witnessed the awesome power and presence of God. We have also experienced growth and increased faith in our individual and personal relationship with God. A response is needed. What will be your response?

Resultant Transformation

Through the years, I have engaged in spirited discussions about whether people can change. That is the foundation of this writing. Again, the transformation is about change. I indicated earlier in this chapter that there are some who believe that they cannot accept Christ into their lives until they are "cleaned up". What a huge misconception! Christ tells us to come as we are. We are invited to do so because we are incapable of cleaning up or transforming ourselves. As we have also previously discussed, the bookstores are replete with self-help books, audio, video, and other materials that tell you how to improve yourself, overcome and get rid of bad habits, and adopt new habits—all as part of a DIY transformation. While there are some things we must do and can do, it is the transforming power of the Holy Spirit at work in our lives that brings about the ability, the initiative, and the power to effect transformation.

If you haven't experienced transformation in any area of your life, I invite you right now to face the mirror and see what's there. Is salvation needed as a first step? Is repentance needed for things you have done to other people, or grief you have caused them, or forgiveness for what others may have done to you? What do you see as you face the mirror?

Mirror, Mirror:
What Reflection Do You See?

Questions for Thought and Reflection:

1. Have you ever been the subject of discussions about your 'slip hanging', or your 'business being in the street'? How did that make you feel?

2. How do you respond to seeing others with their 'slip hanging', or 'business in the street'? Do you pray, counsel them, laugh, or gossip about them or have some other response?

3. Can you recall a time where you repented of something and found deliverance and freedom from that sin? How can your testimony help others?

Chapter 4

Validation Addiction

The Snow-White Conundrum

THERE ARE MANY variations of the well-known fairytale *Snow White and the Seven Dwarfs*: in text form, which originated with the Grimm brothers, or movies, such as the Disney-animated *Snow White*. While there are many variations, the core message is the same concerning the actions and behaviors of Snow White's stepmother, the Queen.

The Queen stood before the mirror each day and asked the same question: "Mirror, Mirror on the wall, who's the fairest of them all?" Day after day, week after week, month after month, year after year, the mirror would reply, "My Queen, you are the fairest one of all." The Queen loved her mirror and how it lifted her spirits. It appeased her mind. It soothed her soul. It validated her, giving her comfort and assurance to get through her day. The mirror affirmed who she was and all that she thought herself to be. The mirror told her what she wanted to hear and saw in her what she wanted seen.

One day, the Queen stood before the mirror that she had trusted for so long. The Queen held the highest rank in the land, with vast power and control at her command. Yet, she kept repeating the same question: "who's the fairest one of all?" Although she expected nothing new or different, she still needed to be validated, for that was what energized her and reassured her of her beauty and worth. She waited for the usual response, but the mirror replied, "Most high Queen, you are indeed beautiful, but there is one fairer than you."

The Queen was not only shocked but also enraged at the mirror's response. It was not what she expected to hear, nor was it what she wanted to hear. A great fury arose and exploded like a ruptured volcano that had been waiting to release its lava and disgorge its' internal conflict and deep-seated emotions. She showed her innermost being shaped over the course of many years by a compounded slew of unsettled and unresolved emotions. These emotions had been suppressed and quieted by the affirming words of the mirror.

While the Queen's external demeanor had exuded great poise and charm, when an unexpected event disrupted her expectations, her inner self came out. Much like the way we put our "game face" on when we face the world. A person's outer behavior is not always aligned with one's inner being. When an internal conflict exists, subconsciously, it is carried by our emotions. Like the illustration of the Queen's emotions, we too may at times appear calm and put-together on the surface, while our internal emotions may be a fiendish mixture of life's experiences that we have suppressed. It is like sweeping dirt under the rug. Only so much dirt can be swept under the rug before it begins to show around the edges. It is the same with our emotions. We can only carry so much before telltale signs began to appear. These may appear on the surface as unexplainable rudeness, anger, criticism, jealousy, unforgiveness, fear, guilt, immorality, mental or psychological disorders. Like the Queen's sudden outburst, when emotional distresses are left unchecked and undealt with, it is only a matter of time before a "trigger" will cause an eruption. We too may carry emotions that when left unattended, will at some point be aroused and erupt where we are exposed and forced to deal with these underlying issues. This capacity may be in all of us—like an active volcano, displaying an outer beauty of mountainous peaks and picturesque scenery, but inside ready at any moment to disgorge molten lava and volcanic gases.

Beware of the Trigger

When certain events or conditions manifest themselves, they may trigger an emotional response that is set loose. It is most likely when you are forced to hear something you have been turning a deaf ear to, or you finally see what you have ignored for far too long. It's like when you have an infected nerve in your gums; when you eat something that is too hot or too cold and it hits that nerve, a sharp pain erupts that is beyond your control. You can try and chew on the other side, but at some point, you cannot avoid or dodge it. You must deal with it!

A trigger can be anything that causes a sudden reaction. A doctor may test your reflexes by using a plexor, better known as a small rubber hammer, to hit a spot just below the kneecap. One quick tap on the "sweet spot" will cause a rapid reaction by the neuromuscular system and thereby trigger nerve receptors which we see as a knee jerk response. While our bodies are much more complex than what is described here, the point made is that a trigger will generally cause a sudden, unexpected, and somewhat uncontrolled response. A trigger causes the release of emotions with force. A trigger can be a person. It can be something said, or something that someone does that reminds you of a time or event in your life that created an emotional disturbance. If you haven't faced the fact that there may be unresolved issues in your life, then the trigger will at some point expose those emotions that have been formed as a result of sweeping them under the carpet.

Like the volcano, when something in us is triggered, the automatic response releases all those deep-seated emotions. It reaches deep within to the place where it first began. These suppressed and unresolved negative experiences and emotions have piled on top of others to act like molten lava, waiting to erupt. The more "stuff" we have compounded through the years, the greater the eruption.

Have you ever witnessed someone who seemed to "fly off the handle" at a small provocation? Sometimes it may not even be a provocation, but the person will respond as though it was. What caused that anger to erupt? It may be a subconscious recollection of something that sparked initial anger that has now turned into hostility. If it's jealousy, it may stem from constant rejection or infidelity in a relationship—married or single. If it is incessant criticism, it may be a learned behavior from a parent, teacher, or influential person, failure, or unresolved dissatisfaction about some aspect of your own life. Whatever the exhibited behaviors are, it is incumbent upon us to explore the root cause and not just treat the symptom. There is something to be appreciated about doctors who look beyond the most-visible symptom and attempt to get to the root cause of the problem to bring complete healing.

While the exhibited behavior is a concern, it is not the real issue. The behavior is only an indication that there is a more profound problem deeply rooted within. It's like when we have a headache. It could be because we are hungry. It could be related to allergies, stress, tension, or a host of other factors. However, the symptom exists to alert us that there is a problem. Likewise, these triggered behaviors are indicators that there is an inner, perhaps deeply-suppressed emotion that must be explored and dealt with. Getting to the core is the only way to bring complete deliverance, healing, spiritual peace, and, moreover, transformation.

Unquenched Validation

The process of validation, in some realms or professions, is essential. For example, when a doctor prescribes more tests, maybe a blood test or x-ray, to gather evidence and makes a diagnosis, the results might validate the doctor's suspicions. Scientists of all types also look for validation of their theories. We also have social validation. We all need to be encouraged, esteemed, and supported as a natural part of healthy relationships. Validation from others can give us the necessary boost to press through difficult situations, or as we embark on new adventures.

The online blog *Psychology Today* provides some additional insights about the term validation. *Psychology Today* sees it as a "means to express understanding and acceptance of another person's internal experience, whatever that might be, not that you necessarily agree or approve. With this perspective, validation can help in building relationships and ease upset feelings. Knowing that you are understood and that others consider your emotions and thoughts is powerful. Validation is like relationship glue."[9]

But what happens when a person doesn't get this type of validation? Or what happens when a person becomes dependent on this kind of validation? What occurs when a person uses validation to constantly satisfy emotions, or as a means of disregarding some valid factors that need addressing? Dr. Michael Hurd, an independent psychotherapist, agrees that the real issue linked to one's internal emotional state is knowing "how they think and feel, as well as how they act in countless small ways in daily life. With the possible exception of a spouse or romantic partner, nobody is as well acquainted with ourselves as... ourselves."[10]

An unhealthy dependency on validation can become a major problem. It is when validation becomes the reliance upon external sources to approve and agree with an individual which legitimizes ones own thoughts and approval of themselves. We might seek it to justify ourselves and our actions in the absence of objectivity. *Snow White*'s Queen was addicted to validation. Every day she sought her mirror and was

---

9 Karyn Hall, "Pieces of Mind: Self-Validation," *Psychology Today,* July 12, 2014, at https://www.psychologytoday.com/blog/pieces-mind/201407/self-validation.
10 Michael Hurd, "Facebook, Social Media and the Psychology of Validation," DrHurd.com, March 16, 2016, at https://drhurd.com/2016/03/16/58528/.

invigorated by the response that she wanted to hear. The Queen relied on the mirror to confirm, approve, and to validate her thoughts of herself. But when the answer, albeit a truthful one, was contrary to what she wanted to hear, she vehemently reacted. Not only was it problematic for her, but she also made it everybody else's problem too, casting the blame.

Can you think of anybody in your life with similar characteristics? I confess that there have been times in my own life where my approach to problem-solving was to call several of my closest friends, one at a time, and get their input regarding a matter and then make my decision. Or worse, to call my friends to get them to agree with me and justify my feelings and actions. I have also seen and experienced situations where people did something that was ethically or morally questionable. When brought to their attention, not only did they justify their actions, they became quite offended; some even became enraged because I did not agree with their position or behavior. I have further witnessed where people would talk to anybody with a listening ear and tell only their side of the story, in order to seek validation. There are always people who will agree with you no matter what you have done. There are also people who will agree with you because they have only heard your side of the story. What if they had the benefit of hearing all the parties, and could make a fully informed decision? Would you want that? Is it truth you seek, or just validation?

Whose Report

I remember a lesson taught by a pastor many years ago. He emphasized that we are to run to God amid trouble or uncertainty, not run away from God. Nor are we to try and hide from God or fix every problem we encounter on our own without wise counsel. Scripture tells us that God is ready to help in times of need. When we run from person to person to confide in them, we are, in essence, running from God. It's like those times in my life when I called my friends to gain support, validation, confidence, or advice, and each time I heard a voice in my spirit-being saying, whose report will you believe?

There are still times when I talk to my friends, but I talk to God first by praying and seeking His guidance through scripture. Putting God first brought about a significant change in my life, as I then began to see his presence and power. Getting answers to prayers builds confidence and trust in God. We learn that He is always present, He is faithful to perform His word, and that we can put our trust in Him. While it is certainly not wrong to talk to others about your challenges or situations you may face, know that there is a difference between seeking wise counsel and seeking unhealthy validation. The biggest difference is straightforwardness. In the search for validation, you are looking for someone to agree with you, or to defend your actions and beliefs, regardless of what they may be. Wise counsel is the truth, be it in agreement with you or not. So, every time I had a desire to get an opinion from my friends, I began to pray first. The results have been remarkable. The validation of the Lord, I have found, leaves me well settled and less troubled than the input of various friends and associates.

God wants us to cast our cares and burdens on Him because He cares for us. God wants us to seek Him. Psalm 118:8 says, "It is better to trust in the LORD than to put confidence in man" (KJV). Further, when we are seeking understanding or direction, one of my favorite and well-known Scriptures is "Trust in the LORD with all thine heart; and lean not unto thine own understanding. In all thy ways acknowledge him, and he shall direct thy paths" (Proverbs 3:5–6 KJV). It took me a few years to learn to do this.

Mirror, Mirror:
What Reflection Do You See?

Questions for Thought and Reflection:

1. What has been your experience with triggers? Have you witnessed a trigger effect in someone else? Have you experienced a trigger in your life?

2. When you look in the mirror, do you see a person who is seeking self-validation, or do you see a person who is seeking truth?

3. If it is the truth you are seeking, are you ready to make changes? Are you ready to put off the old person and to put on the new that is more aligned with the reflection of Christ Jesus?

Chapter 5
Ethical Dilemmas

*Trust in the LORD with all your heart, and do
not lean on your own understanding.
In all your ways acknowledge him, and he
will make straight your paths.*

PROVERBS 3:5

Questionable Actions

A SPOUSE RATIONALIZES AN adulterous relationship because the home life is not satisfying. Instead of working through this situation, the spouse has chosen to seek satisfaction outside of the marriage. They justify their actions by saying, "nothing is happening on the home front."

A business markets a product knowing that there are product defects. The business only cares about its profits and revenue with disregard for consumer protection.

The Pastor of a small independent church establishes a committee to raise funds to build a new church. The church raised enough money and purchased a plot of land outright. Fundraising continued for a few more years to acquire enough cash for a hefty down payment on the construction. The Pastor shows up at church in a brand new 550S Mercedes Benz. After inquiries by church members, they discovered that the funds collected and saved for the new church were used by the Pastor to purchase his new car which he felt entitled to because he founded the church.

As a former state Ethics Commissioner, I can attest that there are ethics violations committed out of ignorance without careful thought. There are also many situations and circumstances where a person is fully aware but attempts to rationalize and justify their actions with claims that they are completely legitimate. Then there are some who think that they can "beat the system." For some, we must ask, "does the end justify the means?"

Think of the people confronted by the prophet Amos. Some had prospered by swindling land from the rightful owners and some by secretly stacking the scales when selling produce and other goods. They prospered, but at the expense of others. When they looked at the riches they had acquired, they thought they were blessed by God. However, their questionable actions clearly violated God's covenant agreement. We discussed the Biblical story of Sapphira and Ananias in chapter two. In summary, the couple sold their land and gave part of the profits to the Disciples to support the ministry work. While they were under no obligation to give any of it, it was deceitful pretense to make it appear as though they gave **all** of what they acquired from the sale to make themselves appear more noble by doing a great deed.

Sometimes these situations and others seem to justify questionable actions. But, is it right for a man to steal a loaf of bread because his family is without food? Is adultery justifiable if a spouse is nonconsenting? Is it admissible to use power and influence, such as in a work position, to cause harm to someone you fear or dislike or for selfish gain? Life is full of perplexing situations and requires morally conscientious thinking and wise decision-making. There have been theological studies and secular discussions about people's actions and life situations and their consequences. Are these conditions clearly black or white? Are they right or wrong, or somewhere in between? And if they aren't so clear, how do we then interpret these ambiguous areas of life? Life can appear complicated and intensifies our search for answers. Like the song, "Looking for love in all the wrong places," many times, we look for answers in all the wrong places. We look for answers in books, videos, talk shows, or the Internet. We seek counsel from our friends, clergy, or sometimes from complete strangers to clarify situations that fall somewhere between the black and the white in areas called, the many shades of gray. It is no surprise to see our clergy, theologians, judges, politicians, ethics commissioners, and others in a continual debate about the gray areas: what is right or wrong, and what is acceptable or unacceptable.

Rightfully so, many have turned to the scriptures to seek answers, understanding and guidance. While this is what we should aspire to do on a regular basis, it is alarming to see on the rise a teaching method that encourages the believer to interpret the scripture based on their own personal understanding. This leads to what theologians call, "*Eisegesis,*" which is simply an interpretation based on is how a person sees it through their lenses and is based on experiential learnings. [11] Perhaps, that is why and how we get so many different perspectives and interpretations of Scripture. Something may appear immoral or unethical to one person, but another may have no moral or ethical issue with it at all. Such approaches minimize critical and systematic processes in interpreting Biblical passages and other literary writings useful in the discovery of their original meaning. This method is known as a hermeneutical or exegetical approach. The word exegesis comes from the Greek word exēgeisthai, meaning to explain, lead out of, or interpret. Absent

---

11 "Exegesis and Eisegesis Definition," The Bible Study Site, at www.biblestudy.org/beginner/definition-of-christian- terms/exegesis.html.

the use of a hermeneutical approach, Scripture can be reduced to mean whatever you want it to say, which opens the door for compromise.

The Door to Compromise

If not the single root cause, compromise is a key element in unethical behavior. Compromise is rampant and has become a silent destroyer of moral aptitude. It is when one's unregenerate nature does what comes naturally. Sometimes it is without thought, guilt, or question, because it is driven by a desire to indulge the needs of the flesh nature and to be satisfied. The incessant desire to satisfy the needs and wants of the flesh, be they material, emotional, physical, or psychological overshadows any sense of moral conscience. We might even think this is the will of God. Or, if we recognize a sinful pattern, we justify our actions and may say, "God made me this way."

The late comedian Flip Wilson was well-known for his infamous one-liner: "the devil made me do it," "the devil made me do it." There may be some truth to that statement; however, we are ultimately responsible for our actions. Compromise may involve actions that the world sees as commonplace and acceptable. However, those who profess Christianity fall prey to the world's moral turpitude, but then face humiliation and disgrace in the public eye when exposed. We may go to church and seek to live a godly life, but if we choose a lifestyle, even if it is acceptable by worldly standards, we may compromise Godly principles. The danger lies in the fact that any compromise can become habitual. The compromised behavior then becomes the norm, giving rise to further compromises and a continual degradation of moral character. This behavior becomes a new normal.

There is a broad spectrum when defining the meaning of the word compromise. Among its many meanings, at one end of that spectrum dictionary.com defines the word compromise as "a means to settle a dispute by mutual concession, or an adjustment of conflicting or opposing claims, or principles." While at the other end, it means, "to make a dishonorable or shameful concession."[12] It is an intermediate state between conflicting opinions, or actions, reached by mutual concession or modification. In the Jewish legal system, while there are various ways that disputes may be resolved, one preferred way of settling a dispute is 'peshara', or arbitration, in which the disputants bring their case to a set number of judges who determine the results based on compromise rather than the strict judgment of the law.

On one hand, compromise is what makes our relationships with others pleasant. Compromise is what makes marital relationships respectable and enduring. Compromise is being able to negotiate and resolve differences or find some middle ground where all parties can agree. Maybe a husband and wife agree to Friday night being their date night. They each commit to keeping their calendars open so that they can spend time together. But what if the wife likes going to the Kennedy Center, the ballet and Broadway shows but the husband likes professional sports and prefer football, basketball, or soccer games. Compromise is needed to avoid continual conflict. Both parties work together to seek a viable solution where both are satisfied in some way. Maybe they agree to go to the Kennedy Center and a professional sports game once a month. Other Friday nights may consist of a movie, dinner out on the town, bowling or just staying home together. This type of compromise is needed in marriages, the home, the workplace and in our churches.

There is however, another side of compromise. It can present itself at the core of situational ethics. When we lower our standards to accommodate worldly ideologies or desires of the flesh that conflict with biblical teachings, we compromise in unfruitful ways. The biblical text tells us that, "Whoever knows the right thing to do and fails to do

---

12 http://www.dictionary.com/browse/compromise

it, for him it is sin" (James 4:17). A biblical illustration of compromise and its consequences can be found in the story of Samson and Delilah.

The Old Testament book of Judges recounts the story of Samson's relationship with Delilah. Samson, an Israelite, was given supernatural strength by God to be used to conquer the Philistines, a continued thorn in the side of Israel. He was also a Nazirite. Samson was dedicated from birth to serve God all the days of his life. A Nazirite could not touch a dead body, had to abstain from wine and grapes and had to avoid cutting his hair or shaving. Samson indulged in a relationship with a Philistine woman, Delilah. This relationship went against all the teachings of his upbringing. For him, there was excitement and pleasure. Perhaps unbeknownst to him was that he was trapped in a sinful relationship filled with lust, deception, vanity, temptation, and—worst of all—compromise. After numerous attempts by Delilah to find the source of his strength, Samson revealed it to her. Delilah betrayed him and led him first to his spiritual death, defeat, and suffering. It ultimately led to his physical death. Samson was deceived because he compromised himself in his relationship with God and suffered because of his choices and actions.

As Christians, we have choices and options. We serve a sovereign God, and we serve Him because we choose to do so out of our own free will. In our modern-day world, do we bend because society expects us to? Do we compromise our values and biblical teachings because we want to fit in? Are we afraid that we might be laughed at, or ridiculed because we refuse to compromise in our biblical teachings?

The story of Daniel is a classic illustration of standing firm in one's relationship with God. It is an example of how compromise could have been a culturally acceptable alternative but commitment to Yahweh prevailed. Daniel, Chapter 3, describes the account of the golden image constructed by King Nebuchadnezzar: huge, measuring sixty cubits by six cubits. This is approximately nine feet in width by ninety feet in height. It was overlaid with pure gold, and even perhaps by modern standards, it seems to have been a monument to behold.[13]

Nebuchadnezzar was one of the most powerful rulers in history. "He dominated the world of his day. He ruled for forty years, and, as a military commander, he never lost a battle. His authority was absolute."[14] The biblical text unveils the series of events that were meant to bring honor to the king but clashed with the Hebraic teachings of the three Hebrew men. "King Nebuchadnezzar sent to gather the satraps, the prefects, and the governors, the counselors, the treasurers, the justices, the magistrates, and all the officials of the provinces to come to the dedication of the image that King Nebuchadnezzar had set up" (Daniel 3:2). All those summoned to appear for the unveiling were there and in place, including the three Hebrew men, Shadrach, Meshach, and Abednego. The image was erected in the plain of Dura, which was a province of the great city Babylon. The plain was wide open, where the image could be prominently seen for miles away without obstruction. As the people gathered, the ceremony appears to have been brief and to the point:

And the herald proclaimed aloud, "You are commanded, O peoples, nations, and languages, that when you hear the sound of the horn, pipe, lyre, trigon, harp, bagpipe, and every kind of music, you are to fall down and worship the golden image that King Nebuchadnezzar has set up. And whoever does not fall down, and worship shall immediately be cast into a burning fiery furnace." Therefore, as soon as all the peoples heard the sound of the horn, pipe, lyre, trigon, harp, bagpipe, and every kind of music, all the peoples, nations, and languages fell down and worshiped the golden image that King Nebuchadnezzar had set up" (Daniel 3:4–7).

The instructions were clear. The king exerted his authority and provided an ultimatum, bow or burn! The air was filled with pageantry,

---

13 John F. Walvoord, "The Golden Image of Nebuchadnezzar," *Daniel: The Key to Prophetic Revelation*, January 1, 2008, at www.Bible.org/seriespage/Chapter-3-golden-image-nebuchadnezzar.
14 Marvin J. Rosenthal, "Zion's Fire," *The Conquest of Babylon* 23, no. 6 (July–August 2012): 7–9.

and the people stood ready to comply with the instructions. As the instruments sounded with pomp and circumstance, all the people bowed and worshiped the golden image—except the three Hebrew men who remained standing. They had a choice, and they chose not to bow, instead opting to hold fast to the teachings of God. Although they understood the alternative, they refused to compromise.

I thought about what I would do. Would I have bowed? Everyone else bowed. Perhaps the consequence of not bowing was a strong motive. Peer pressure is one thing. Societal pressure that flows from the highest position in the land is certainly another and worthy of careful thought. In this case the consequence of not bowing was death in the fiery furnace. We may quickly assert that we would have stood firm. However, if we consider our current day societal pressures where physical death is not a consequence, how much do we hold fast to Godly principles? When we consider the pressure to conform to cultural standards and accept diverse ideologies, or practice tolerance to worldly beliefs and philosophies, I ask, what would you do?

The instructions handed down by King Nebuchadnezzar were the customs of the day. They did not present a cultural or religious conflict for the pagan people. But the instructions brought conflict for the Hebrew men. They resolved that the decree was contrary to the teachings of the Hebrew Scriptures and the God they served but nonetheless, chose to adhere to the instruction of the Pentateuch, in Exodus 20:4–5: "You shall not make for yourself a carved image or any likeness of anything that is in heaven above, or that is in the earth beneath, or that is in the water under the earth. You shall not bow down to them or serve them, for I the Lord your God am a jealous God." This may have been seen as antiquated, or not applicable in this circumstance since they had been seized and transported from their homeland of Judah during the Babylonian captivity. There is a vernacular that says, "When in Rome, do as the Romans do." The questions that should be raised, however, are, what are the Romans doing? And, who are you? Just because the rest of the world is doing it, does not make it right before God. The biblical text indicates that it was not difficult to see or recognize that these three did not bow:

"Therefore, at that time certain Chaldeans came forward and maliciously accused the Jews. They declared to King Nebuchadnezzar, "O king, live forever! You, O king, have made a decree, that every man who hears the sound of the horn, pipe, lyre, trigon, harp, bagpipe, and every kind of music, shall fall down and worship the golden image. And whoever does not fall down, and worship shall be cast into a burning fiery furnace. There are certain Jews whom you have appointed over the affairs of the province of Babylon: Shadrach, Meshach, and Abednego. These men, O king, pay no attention to you; they do not serve your gods or worship the golden image that you have set up." (Daniel 3:8–12)

With seemingly-malicious intent, the Chaldeans informed the king that the Hebrews did not obey the decree. "They remind the king that these men are Jews, different in race and culture from the Babylonians. The king reigned over the affairs of the province of Babylon, the most important province in the empire and the key to political security for the entire realm. The personal loyalty of such officers should be beyond question; but, as the Chaldeans point out, Shadrach, Meshach, and Abednego had not shown any regard for the king himself."[15]

We can only speculate as to why the Chaldeans seemed to be maliciously motivated. It is certainly not unlike what we see in our present day with an increase in attitudes of malice, bigotry, and cultural antagonism.

There are many illustrations throughout scripture that highlight the conflict between the Hebrew people and other cultures. The Chaldean men had previously voiced claims against the Hebrews (Daniel 1:8–21), which could explain why the king asked the three men if it was true what the Chaldeans spoke. Given a second opportunity to bow and worship

---

15 Walvoord, at www.Bible.org/seriespage/Chapter-3-golden-image-nebuchadnezzar.

the image, the Hebrew men again stood firmly with faith and courage and refused to bow. They faced the consequence that Nebuchadnezzar had made clear beforehand of being thrown into a fiery furnace that was heated three times hotter than previously planned.

If the concept of situational ethics had been applied to Shadrach, Meshach, and Abednego, perhaps they would have bowed along with everyone else. There would have been no questions asked. Everyone would have gone back to work or home, and there would have been no story about the overheated fire or how the three Hebrews were bound and thrown into the fiery furnace. There would be no end that has inspired readers for centuries. From the biblical account, the king saw not only the three men who were thrown in but a fourth person in the furnace, unbound and walking around (Daniel 3:24–25).

"Then Nebuchadnezzar came near to the door of the burning fiery furnace; he declared, 'Shadrach, Meshach, and Abednego, servants of the Most High God, come out, and come here!' Then Shadrach, Meshach, and Abednego came out from the fire. And the satraps, the prefects, the governors, and the king's counselors gathered together and saw that the fire had not had any power over the bodies of those men. The hair of their heads was not singed, their cloaks were not harmed, and no smell of fire had come upon them. Nebuchadnezzar answered and said, 'Blessed be the God of Shadrach, Meshach, and Abednego, who has sent his angel and delivered his servants, who trusted in him, and set aside the king's command, and yielded up their bodies rather than serve and worship any god except their own God. Therefore, I make a decree: Any people, nation, or language that speaks anything against the God of Shadrach, Meshach, and Abednego shall be torn limb from limb, and their houses laid in ruins, for there is no other god who can rescue in this way.' Then the king promoted Shadrach, Meshach, and Abednego in the province of Babylon" (Daniel 3:26–30).

Have you ever attempted to imagine what would have happened

if Shadrach, Meshach, and Abednego had bowed and compromised? What is evident to me is that the king and all of his satraps, governors, and other onlookers would have missed an opportunity to see the power of the God of the Hebrew people.

Fitting In

We want to fit in. We want to be a part of the team. But to what extent? In the present day, we are continuously challenged to conform to the culture. We might compromise our values and beliefs in order to fit in, which may cancel out opportunities for others to know the power and might of our God. We might be seen as no different from those 'in the world', and thus, not only miss the mark of being as 'salt of the earth' but also diminish our effectiveness as witnesses for Christ. Even worse, we thwart the plans and purposes of how God wants to use us. We may not always have understanding, but, in faith, we know that God never leaves us or forsakes us (Hebrews 13:5). If we think that it's inconsequential to bow to modern culture, we deceive ourselves, and our testimony becomes ineffectual.

It is trickery of the enemy when we appear to prosper in sin. We think that it must be acceptable because we don't always experience immediate consequences. It is like running a great race with perseverance and commitment. We work hard to reach a goal, only to realize after expending enormous time and energy that we've been running on a treadmill. We have devoted our energy and positive mentality, with high hopes for rewards, when, in the end, we've gotten nowhere. Sin eventually catches up, and sometimes with such overwhelming impact that we are left wondering where it all began. Galatians 6:7–8 says, *"Do not be deceived: God is not mocked, for whatever one sows, that will he also reap. For the one who sows to his flesh will from the flesh reap corruption, but the one who sows to the Spirit will from the Spirit reap eternal life."*

Things may sail smoothly in your life for many years, but continual sin is like sowing seeds of corruption that can only bring forth undesired consequences. As bad seeds grow in one's life, they choke out the Word and drown out good seeds. We must endeavor to sow good seeds to bring forth a harvest reflective of Christendom.

Mirror, Mirror:
What Reflection Do You See?

Questions for Thought and Reflection:

1. Can you think of a situation where you faced an ethical dilemma? Did you seek counsel, or how did you handle the matter?

2. Is there an example of a time when you faced a compromising situation in your spiritual beliefs? What did you do to address it?

3. Can you cite an example of a decision you made and experienced some consequence later, whether it was a good outcome or a learning experience?

Chapter 6

A Clash of Cultures

The kingdom of heaven suffers violence, and the violent take it by force.
—MATTHEW 11:12 NKJV

It's a Clash: Have You Noticed?

OLIVER WENDELL HOLMES Sr. said that "a man's mind, once stretched by a new idea, never regains its original dimensions." I have often wondered what contextual circumstances would prompt someone to write or make such profound statements that are relevant even generations later. Though I may never know or understand, I can from my own experiences attest to the validity of Holmes's statement. His view can apply to worthy and productive ideas as well as evil. Images of immorality dominate our television airways, movie theaters, the Internet, and print media. Programming once thought to be inappropriate for television or radio now bombard our airways. Our minds are saturated with the lyrics of songs that withhold nothing from the imagination.

There is a crafty practice by some, believing that if the American people are continually bombarded with shocking ideologies and images, with continual displays, the people become desensitized and complacent. Though initially shocked, over time, they are no longer outraged or even moved by such suggestions, as they shift their view seeing it as "a way of life." As a result, our moral behaviors continue to decline. Those who do cringe at deplorable images endure labels such as being timid, backward, unsophisticated, or simple! Godly values erode and are compromised and supplanted by a modern-day worldview. I am reminded of the title of a speech I gave some years ago in South Carolina, titled, *"What was once unthinkable has today not only become thinkable, but doable."* This is exactly what we are seeing and experiencing in today's culture.

To explain it simplistically, the current reality that we face is a war of cultural ideologies. Some theologians advocate that there are two distinct, primary worldviews. On the one hand is a worldview defined by a reality grounded in naturalism. On the other, is a reality established upon a transcendent worldview perspective that is rooted in holism. Wikipedia defines naturalism as a philosophical viewpoint according to which everything arises from natural properties and causes, and supernatural or spiritual explanations are excluded or discounted.[16] It is a doctrine, or system of thought that rejects spiritual and supernatural explanations of the world and holds science as the sole basis of what can be known. Science is its foundation, and whatever is known or can be explained or understood becomes a god; that which is unexplainable is rejected.

History was not one of my favorite subjects in high school. I avoided it as much as possible in college. However, during my theological studies, history became my all-time favorite. As an example, one of the most profound periods of humankind's existence illustrating a clashing of cultures was that of Alexander, king of the ancient Greek kingdom of Macedon, perhaps more widely known as Alexander the

---
16 https://simple.wikipedia.org/wiki/Naturalism

Great. The proliferation of the Greek Hellenistic culture and its influence throughout the Mediterranean world changed the face of Middle-Eastern culture to the point that we can still see its impression today. During the reign of Alexander in the third century BC, the Greek culture proliferated throughout his vast empire. By conquest and assimilation, the people, their possessions, and diverse cultures, including Israel, became a part of his kingdom. His goal was to capture the entire known world. Although these various lands instantly came under his rule, they continued to live according to the customs and culture of their land for a season. But it wasn't long before Alexander embraced the idea of unifying the people into one culture, known as Hellenism. His idea transcended the boundaries of the Greek lands and sought to transform his vast empire by making Greek the preferred language, anticipating that after adopting the language the people would unite under a common, unified culture.[17]

The Greek and the Hebraic: Like Clanging Cymbals

Just as we have experienced massive cultural clashes here in the United States, the introduction of the Hellenistic culture within Judah caused great tension and division among the Jews. As Hellenism sank deeper and deeper into the fabric of the Hebraic culture, tension and conflict escalated, creating factions in which those who refused to compromise in their monotheistic beliefs banned together. The more pious ones became known as the Pharisees. The more intellectually cultured Hebrews, who embraced the Greek culture blended it with their own Judaic culture, promoted commerce and trade, and joined forces with Rome in political matters, were the Sadducees. Another group formed and were known as the Zealots.[18] The Jewish Encyclopedia describes

---

17 Calvin J. Roetzel, *The World That Shaped the New Testament* (Atlanta: John Knox Press, 1985), vii, 10, 11–12.
18 Richard Niswonger, *New Testament History* (Grand Rapids, MI: Zondervan, 1988), 24, 236.

the Zealots as those who were "zealous defenders of the Law and of the national life of the Jewish people." The Zealots were a party of Jewish loyalists "opposing with relentless rigor any attempt to bring Judea under the dominion of idolatrous Rome."[19] They were dogmatic in their determination to free Israel of all defilement. Because of the cultural shift from Judaism, to Greek Hellenism, a fourth group called the Essenes was formed. They are a sect known as the Holy Ones. The Essenes retreated from the conflict of mainstream society and closed themselves off from the rest of the world. They are believed to have founded a small community in Qumran, just off the northwest coast of the Dead Sea. This region is where the Dead Sea Scrolls were discovered in deserted caves between 1946 and 1956. There is wide belief that the ancient Jewish sect, the Essenes, are responsible for the development of the Dead Sea Scrolls.

While the influence of Greek Hellenism brought about art, music, astrology, diverse philosophies, and scientific discoveries, as well as, the Septuagint Bible, a Greek translation from Hebrew and Aramaic, it also instigated conflict and cultural clashes associated with Jewish monotheistic beliefs. These philosophies and beliefs were causes of tension, confusion, and diverging beliefs in the first-century church of Paul's day among Gentiles and Jews.

Evolution of Ideologies

Many kinds of religions, philosophies, and beliefs have infiltrated our culture today. People from diverse backgrounds with varied experiences, beliefs, teachings, and values come into the church. America has become known as a melting pot and blend of many cultures and ideologies. Just as in Paul's day, Discipleship in our churches is challenged by the various beliefs and ideologies. Congregationalists hold onto their

---

19 Kaufmann Kohler, "Zealots," *Jewish Encyclopedia* (1906), at www.jewishencyclopedia.com/articles/15185-zealots.

mental, spiritual, and emotional attachment to these belief systems. They embrace the doctrine of Jesus Christ but compound it with all the others.

The problem is one of dilution. I call it a dilution of the Word. There are sprinklings of good, and certain aspects of these ideologies are altruistic: love for humankind, respect for nature, or helping others. When trying to counter these beliefs, we may not recognize the cause of the problem. Without understanding the root cause of what we see, we merely treat the symptoms. The Apostle Paul reminds us in Ephesians 5:6, "Let no one deceive you with empty words, for because of these things the wrath of God comes upon the sons of disobedience." There are impending consequences to those who follow deception and lies. A publication titled, "The Rebirth of America," carefully illustrates the results of buying into a humanistic agenda: "When a Nation listens to the lie … It dethrones God and acclaims man's achievements. It exalts human reason as supreme. It trusts education and science [and money] to solve its problems. It believes that man is evolving into perfection. It replaces God's moral standards with situational ethics. It promotes sensual pleasure and instant gratification. It strives for a world utopia of prosperity and peace. It makes the State the sovereign dictator over everyone." [20]

A passage from the book of Jeremiah further emphasizes this point, making clear where we are to place our confidence and also the consequences of following the errant ideologies:

> *Cursed is the one who trusts in man,*
> *who depends on flesh for his strength and*
> *whose heart turns away from the LORD.*
> *He will be like a bush in the wastelands;*
> *he will not see prosperity when it comes.*
> *He will dwell in the parched places of the desert,*
> *in a salt land where no one lives.*

---

[20] Nancy Leigh DeMoss, ed., *The Rebirth of America* (Philadelphia: Arthur S. DeMoss Foundation 1986), 144.

But blessed is the man who trusts in the LORD,
whose confidence is in him.
He will be like a tree planted by the water
that sends out its roots by the stream.
It does not fear when heat comes;
its leaves are always green.
It has no worries in a year of drought and
never fails to bear fruit. (Jeremiah 17:5–8 NIV)

Divergent Worldviews

Several years ago, I attended the Ninth Annual Conference on Apologetics, Evangelism, and Human Rights in Strasbourg, France. One of the lecturers, Dr. Oliver H. G. Wilder-Smith, who was at that time, an assistant professor at the Radboud University Medical Centre, in Nijmegen, Netherlands, set forth a perspective of these current realities. He eloquently differentiated a transcendent worldview from a naturalistic worldview. In summary, he noted that a transcendent worldview is one defined by a reality above and beyond the limits of material experience or human sense perception. It is knowable through revelation. Christianity declares that all of nature and creation has a supernatural and divine explanation from its origin, described in the book of Genesis. It views the natural order as evidence for the existence of God; the universe and its laws, including scientific and ethical, providing humankind with a profound revelation of God's existence.

The account of the parable of the wheat and tares illustrates these opposing worldviews. The Gospel of Matthew 13:24–43 presents the parable in two parts. The first part provides insights to reality—that there are two opposing forces at work in the world that bear some similarities but are vastly different. Part 1 of the parable is described in verses 24–30:

> "He put another parable before them, saying, "The kingdom of heaven may be compared to a man who sowed good seed in his field, but while his men were sleeping, his enemy came and sowed weeds among the wheat and went away. So when the plants came up and bore grain, then the weeds appeared also. And the servants of the master of the house came and said to him, 'Master, did you not sow good seed in your field? How then does it have weeds?' He said to them, 'An enemy has done this.' So the servants said to him, 'Then do you want us to go and gather them?' But he said, 'No, lest in gathering the weeds you root up the wheat along with them. Let both grow together until the harvest, and at harvest time I will tell the reapers, Gather the weeds first and bind them in bundles to be burned, but gather the wheat into my barn."

In the second part of the parable, Jesus offers a response and interpretation as His disciples ask for understanding of its meaning. This is the interpretation as provided by the Lord Jesus to the disciples and for all today:

> "Then he left the crowds and went into the house. And his disciples came to him, saying, "Explain to us the parable of the weeds of the field." He answered, "The one who sows the good seed is the Son of Man. The field is the world, and the good seed is the sons of the kingdom. The weeds are the sons of the evil one, and the enemy who sowed them is the devil. The harvest is the close of the age, and the reapers are angels. Just as the weeds are gathered and burned with fire, so will it be at the end of the age. The Son of Man will send his angels, and they will gather out of his kingdom all causes of sin and all law-breakers and throw them into the fiery furnace. In that place, there will be weeping and gnashing of teeth. Then the righteous will shine like the sun in the kingdom of their Father. He who has ears, let him hear" (Matthew 13:36–43).

My research into wheat and tares yielded diverse perspectives of how the two plants bear remarkable similarities in the earlier stage of developing and sprouting; even the most discerning eye might be challenged to distinguish between them. But as they mature, the wheat takes on a much different look and size. We might surmise that this is the reason both were allowed to grow together until the time of harvesting when the tares would be more evident and could then be gathered and thrown into the fire. The wheat could easily be mistaken for a tare if the tares were pulled too soon. Further, the growing root system of the tare can wrap its roots around the wheat, making it difficult and perhaps impossible to remove the tare independently of the wheat. They both must coexist together until the time of harvesting when they would then be separated.

An article by Alan Yusko, "Tares and Wheat: Everyone Is Showing Their True Colour," describes the "wheat" as the person who is truly saved and born again; Yusko purports that the tare represents those who claim to be Christian. "They look like a Christian, and sometimes they act like a Christian. Tares go to Christian churches, and some rise in leadership to be deacons, elders, and pastors ... The tare claims to be a Christian and would get very angry if told otherwise and sometimes, it may be difficult to differentiate them from the worldly."[21]

In part 2 of the parable, Jesus makes clear that the message is about people. It is an illustration of those who confess and obey and those who simply confess a belief in God. It also illustrates the progressive nature of spiritual transformation. We do not become spiritual giants or mature saints overnight. It is a gradual change achieved through a continual commitment and obedience to God's Word with an earnest desire to grow in knowledge and relationship with Christ Jesus.

---

21 Alan Yusko, *"Tares and Wheat: Everyone Is Showing Their True Colour,"* http://heaven77.50webs.com/whtare03.html.

Scripture indicates that some visible signs and attributes show a person's true nature—that is, a person's inner life that reflects outwardly shows one's true colors, not just one's hypocritical words, sometimes even preached from the pulpit. The tares are those who call themselves Christian but cling to the old life, doing the will of the flesh.

For those who live according to the flesh set their minds on the things of the flesh, but those who live according to the Spirit set their minds on the things of the Spirit. For to set the mind on the flesh is death, but to set the mind on the Spirit is life and peace. For the mind that is guided by the flesh is hostile to God, for it does not submit to God's law; indeed, it cannot. Those who are in the flesh cannot please God. (Romans 8:5–8)

Like the Queen in Snow White, when pushed to the limits of trials and tribulations, the true colors within are exposed. When matters didn't go her way or, more pointedly, when the mirror reflected her true identity from within, she didn't submit to and accept the truth. Rather, she revolted in outraged anger, fury, jealousy, bitterness, and even retaliation. We, too, may face a trial or temptation at some point in our walk with God. It may simply be a time of testing, or it may be to identify something that God wants to change and or mature within us.

Further, the parable speaks of gathering the wheat into the barn. Before it can reach this point, it must be winnowed on the threshing floor. There are numerous mentions of the threshing floor, mostly in the Old Testament. It is a place of separating grain from the chaff. Matthew 3:12 states that "His winnowing fork is in his hand, and he will clear his threshing floor and gather his wheat into the barn, but the chaff he will burn with unquenchable fire."

So, while some may look like disciples of Christ and may talk a good game, it is unquestionably the winnowing process and the threshing floor that will shine light and separate those who walk in truth from those who are imposters (Matthew 7:15). The winnowing process entails beating the wheat against a hard surface such as stone, vigorous shaking, pulling, and ultimately ensuring that it is free from any chaff. Symbolically speaking, when that grain is ready to be used for baking, the last thing you want is for it to be polluted with rocks or unwanted debris.

We too may experience at intervals a testing of our faith, our character, our commitment to God and obedience to his word. Sometimes we show our true nature and character when challenges arise. If someone wrongs me, do I quickly seek revenge? If I am overlooked for a promotion or a raise, do I become bitter and decide that I am going to only do just enough to get by and no more? If someone curses me, do I give them a dose of their own and then some?

We may be guilty ourselves, or perhaps we have known someone who professed Christianity, but when the first trial came, they quickly returned to the way they'd always known.

The parable of the wheat and tares vividly illustrates two worldviews that are diametrically opposed to each other but coexist together, in the same space. Numerous worldviews and sub-views may be called many names, such as humanism, secularism, existentialism, naturalism, liberalism, realism, paganism, or just plain ole' heathenism. No matter what "ism" it may be or what name is used, all are in opposition to the other side, that being a biblical worldview, one that is transcendent and rooted in holism. It is where God stands and rules supreme, and humankind lives in submission to His holy ordinances.

Steve Gallagher emphasizes the condition of the church today in his book, *Intoxicated with Babylon*. Gallagher stresses that "the church today is so intoxicated with worldly influences and blinded by materialism that holism falls precipitously low."[22] Like the parable of the

---

22 Gallagher, Steve, *Intoxicated with Babylon*, (Kentucky: Lockman Foundation, 1996). P. 11.

wheat and tares, it begs the question, what seeds are you planting today in the lives of others, intentionally or subconsciously? While we cannot control the lives of others—what they think or do, or even how they perceive one's benevolent intention—we must ask ourselves:

Mirror, Mirror:
What Reflection Do You See?

Questions for Thought and Reflection:

1. Does the confession of my faith line up with the way I live? Is my character aligned, or is it being aligned, with that of Christ Jesus?

2. Can you identify how a cultural clash has affected your growth in the Lord?

3. How have you overcome?

4. In what way does the parable of the wheat and the tares relate to your own life?

Chapter 7

A Looking Glass for Others

A True Model

I AM BLESSED TO have had the influence of phenomenal women in my life. When I was about twelve years old, I was intrigued by my Mother Clarice. She was a quiet and soft-spoken woman who spoke volumes of wisdom. My fascination, however, was with her sense of style and her shapely figure. As a preteen and late into my teenage years, I was rail thin, much smaller than my peers. I weighed less than a hundred pounds, had no curvature and still wore "training" bras. My classmates teased me incessantly. Needless to say, I had not blossomed yet. To be more exact, I looked like I had not even begun the process. It also didn't help that I was two years ahead of my peers, having started first grade at the age of four. I was fifteen entering my senior year in high school.

As I considered Mother Clarice's mature and shapely figure, I wondered how she'd gotten that figure. One day, as I was browsing through the encyclopedias on her bookcase, I ran across a large, picture-filled book by Jack LaLanne, titled Jack LaLanne's Slim and Trim Diet and Exercise Guide (1969). I was most intrigued by his plan on how to exercise your way to a Perfect Shape. It was as if I had just discovered a diamond mine. My first thought was "Aha! This is it! This is how she got that perfect shape."

So, I secretly borrowed her book, and, for the next thirty days, I was on a mission. Every day after school, I rushed home to do my Jack LaLanne exercises. I worked extra hard on my legs to make my calves bigger and more muscular. I also did double the exercises on my upper body. Need I be more specific? I was so excited about the potential for a newfound figure, and although I didn't know or understand Scripture, I had "faith." I fully expected drastic and amazing results in thirty days. So, as you can imagine, the thirty-day mark arrived quickly; and I was perplexed as to why I did not yield the results I fully expected. In fact, I showed absolutely no improvement or change whatsoever.

At her birthday celebration of ninety years, Mother Clarice still had that shapely figure. She walked daily, lived a modest lifestyle, and volunteered to serve others. She ate her meals from a saucer instead of a plate, and she looked more like sixty than ninety. Though she never lectured me about the value of exercising or eating smaller meals, her lifestyle, along with her character and nature, spoke to even the most casual observer. While she knew many people in the community, there are so many more who knew her by her steadfast example of Christ. It is shortsighted that our perspective of a model is focused on the external, be it physical beauty, money, or fame with little to no concern about one's inner qualities.

I have also been influenced by Mother Charlene. Though for most of my life she has lived far from me, I know that I have inherited her genes of creativity in dance, writing, and the arts. She too is a woman of great style, eloquence, beauty, and Christian love. I have a friend who once asked me how I came to acquire my sense of style and sophistication. While it is perhaps learned through books, teachings, and mirroring, it must also be a part of my genetic makeup. Sadly,

Mother Clarice transitioned to eternal life on March 10, 2018 just prior to the completion of this book. She will be greatly missed, but her legacy of Christ's Disciple will live on for generations to come.

The Art of Mirroring

There have been numerous studies conducted on various techniques and the effects of "mirroring." These studies give credence to the persuasive effects of social-learning constructs in intimate environments. That is to say, young minds are impressionable and will mimic what they see more than what they hear. Mirroring, in its simplest form, is defined as a behavior that is learned subconsciously through observation and interaction. Sometimes these learned behaviors may not become evident until some years later. I often coach mothers of daughters—and especially teenage daughters—about mother-daughter relationships. I can attest that, while children may show no sign that they are paying attention to you (verbal or nonverbal), they are watching your every move. If you are making positive moves, they too will do so later in life.

I have been surprised by my daughters. Many times, I felt that they were in a world of their own. Into their teenage years, a time when they think they know all about life and set out to prove it, I was amazed by how they mimicked exactly some things they saw me do. My first revelation of this occurred on Mother's Day. It was their idea to cook dinner. They informed me that I could invite a few guests to eat with us. They planned the menu, just as I usually do when planning a special meal for guests. They did the shopping, the cooking, and even set the table as I would have, while adding their individual touches of creativity. I was amazed! Even our guests commented about the exquisitely prepared and served food, and the ambiance encapsulated in a warm, hospitable atmosphere. There had been many times when I had felt they had paid no attention to me or my teachings. Imagine my surprise!

Titus talks about mirroring in a similar way. That is, we are to show ourselves to be a model of good works, in all respects. That means we are to model godly behavior in our integrity. We model godly behavior in our self-control, in our finances, in our sexuality, and in our interactions with others. We are to model godly behavior in how we speak about other people in their presence and behind their backs. We are to model dignity and speak words of exhortation to set an example for others. Though sometimes it may be hard to do with some people, we are yet challenged to live such exemplary lives that a would-be opponent would be put to shame, having nothing evil to say about us (Titus 2:1–8).

There are various modalities of social learning, and the concept of mirroring is one of many. Dr. Lloyd Thomas, in his study, Mirroring, states that "all children learn how to view themselves and how to treat themselves, using two basic methods: imitation of how others treat themselves; and observing how they themselves are treated."[23] He provides an example of how a child who watches a parent engaging in self-abusive behavior may learn, through social-learning constructs, to practice self-abuse. Even with the most innocent conduct, casual observers form perceptions of what they perceive to be part of a "normal" relationship.

Dr. Thomas elaborates on behaviors learned through mirroring: "when children are physically, mentally, or emotionally abused, they learn to hate themselves ... not the abuser."[24] In this mirrored behavior, children learn from the actions of others within their social spheres. Dr. Thomas indicates that their behaviors are shaped by the image they have of others and the perception they learn through personal experience. The impact of mirroring relates not only to children but also extends to adult learning and behavior.

---

[23] Lloyd J. Thomas, *Mirroring*, E-Book, p. 10. http://www.internationalbreathinstitute.com/articles/mirror.htm.
[24] Ibid.

Many examples show how people can become products of their environment as well as producers. Those who become products of an environment are those who adopt the abusive behaviors they experienced and exhibit them in their own lives toward others. Studies show that hurt people often hurt others, especially when bombarded by family conflict on a regular basis. Human development is a lifelong process. Those who become producers of their environment are those who may have also experienced abuse, neglect, ridicule or other traumatic behaviors but, are those who overcome and may even go on to become advocates for change in a cause to fight against what they themselves have experienced.

There are also those who abuse themselves in other ways. There are some who have no care or concern for their health and well-being. They routinely over indulge. Additionally, we feed our minds, through music, movies, or social interactions in unhealthy ways. We justify our actions and behaviors and do nothing to improve. We may recognize an unhealthy relationship but do nothing to change or end that relationship. Just as we discussed in an earlier chapter, we rationalize our behavior, we find reasons to do what we do and convince ourselves that it is acceptable. Here again, this is not a message about perfection, but it is a nudge to face the mirror to exercise empowerment and be all that God has created us to be and to fulfill his purpose in life. Isn't it time to be free, to be overcomers? 1 John 5:4-5 reminds us that *"For everyone who has been born of God overcomes the world. And this is the victory that has overcome the world—our faith. Who is it that overcomes the world except for the one who believes that Jesus is the Son of God?"*

The growth and development of cognitive skills for sound reasoning, decision-making, and maturity are highly dependent on modeled behavior, regardless of age, whether adult to adolescent or adult to adult. As adults, we often continue to serve as mirrors for one another. We look to others to reflect information about ourselves. We seek a particular mentor or coach because we admire some attribute of, or accomplishment by, that person, or we recognize an area in our life that could improve with an accountability partner.

Just as we observe, as I did with so many influential people in my life, many times we are also being observed. Without our having a clue, others watch us from afar and may never interact or communicate with us. They see how we act and react in various situations and how we relate. The world watches those of us who are Christians, neighbors, and acquaintances. Friends observe if our lives align with our talk or beliefs to measure if it connects with the profession of our faith.

The point of this discussion is twofold. The first point is that we learn from modeled behavior, be it productive or toxic. I think of young adults who sometimes emulate highly visible athletes or entertainers as examples of success. Like babies, young impressionable minds model the behaviors they see.

The second point is an objective to set forth the understanding that others are learning from us, be it through direct interaction, or from afar. Did you ever pause to think about what others may see from afar, where there is no verbal communication or interaction? What message are we sending by our behaviors? What are we mirroring to others?

Have you ever been in a heated discussion with someone and they refused to argue with you? They never raised their voice or changed the tone of their voice but continued to discuss the matter driving to a mutual resolution. There is an erosion of our testimony and its impact on the public's view of Christianity when we fail to reflect the Christ-like model that we purport to emulate. There seems to be a continual mockery of the Christian world because the reflection of Christ Jesus grows dim. It appears that when an indiscretion is exposed about someone with high visibility within the Christian community, the world awaits the salacious details while pointing a finger and hurling verbal attacks against all of Christianity. All throughout history, the church has faced ridicule and opposition from those on the outside.

Too many people profess Christianity but have no idea what being a Christian means. A visiting pastor from India spoke at my northern Virginia church. At the very onset of his message, he proclaimed that he did not use the term Christian, explaining that it was a much-overused word whose true meaning had been lost. He preferred to use the term, Disciples of Christ. Regardless of the semantics, as Christians, or Disciples and followers of Christ, we are exhorted to be witnesses for Him in the earthly realm. But what is the testimony of our witness? What is the reflection that we cast? Our lives are to be a model for others and influence what others model.

Naomi's Reflection

Throughout my life, I have been blessed to have so many individuals casting a reflection of Christ Jesus as an example for me. While I thought of names, it could turn out to be an ongoing list akin to the genealogy of Christ in the Gospel of Matthew. On a more serious note, however, I think the biblical story of Ruth is a powerful example of how someone's faithfulness produced positive results in a younger generation. While the biblical text does not provide details about Ruth's upbringing, we do know that she was a Moabite woman who married into a Jewish family of which Naomi was the matriarch. The opening chapter in the Old Testament account of the story of Ruth provides a historic staging of the events to unfold.

> *"In the days when the judges ruled there was a famine in the land, and a man of Bethlehem in Judah went to sojourn in the country of Moab, he and his wife and his two sons. The name of the man was Elimelech and the name of his wife Naomi, and the names of his two sons were Mahlon and Chilion. They were Ephrathites*

from Bethlehem in Judah. They went into the country of Moab and remained there. But Elimelech, the husband of Naomi, died, and she was left with her two sons. These took Moabite wives; the name of the one was Orpah and the name of the other Ruth. They lived there about ten years, and both Mahlon and Chilion died, so that the woman was left without her two sons and her husband" (Ruth 1:1–5).

The story continues, to tell how Naomi resolved to return to her hometown of Bethlehem to be with kin. She implored her daughters-in-law to likewise return to their native homeland. While Orpah did just that, Ruth clung to her mother-in-law Naomi, refusing to leave her.

There is a lot that can be read into the text. We see from the text that Ruth had a home that she could return to since Naomi implored her to go back to her "mother's house" (Ruth 1:8). We could speculate that she would not be welcomed back, seeing that she had married outside of the cultural norms of her day; she was a Moabite woman married to an Israelite man from the tribe of Judah. The history between Moab and Judah was tumultuous at best. The Moabite origin is rooted in the incestuous relationship between Lot and his daughter, whom she named Moab, the father of the Moabites (Genesis 19:36–37). The Moabites worshipped a pantheon of pagan gods, including Chemosh and Baal (Numbers 21:29; 25:3).

From the text, we see that there was a kindred relationship between Naomi and her daughters-in-law. "Naomi said to her two daughters-in-law, 'May the LORD deal kindly with you, as you have dealt with the dead and with me'" (Ruth 1:8). Ruth was unswerving in her determination to follow Naomi, even to the point of forsaking her upbringing and the gods of her land. There was something about Naomi and her God Yahweh that captured the young Moabite woman's heart and soul. Ruth's commitment is clear: "'Do not urge me to leave you or to return from following you. For where you go I will go and where you lodge

I will lodge. Your people shall be my people and your God my God. Where you die I will die, and there will I be buried. May the LORD do so to me and more also if anything but death parts me from you.' And when Naomi saw that she was determined to go with her, she said no more" (Ruth 1:16–18).

Although the religion and culture between Naomi and Ruth were very different, it did not hinder their relationship. It was Naomi's life and her relationship with the God of Abraham, Isaac, and Jacob that similarly drew Ruth. We cannot effectively share our faith with others if all they can see is dirty laundry. We are charged to live quietly and take care of our affairs (1 Thessalonians 4:11). That is, we are to mind our business, spend time growing our relationship with God through prayer, such that we can apply the Word in our daily lives. As we grow and mature in the Lord, then we are better equipped to build sound relationships and where others can see Christ in us.

The overused cliché "if you talk the talk, you must walk the walk" speaks volumes about the reflection we cast and will set forth a powerful example for others of the presence of Christ in our lives.

Mirror, Mirror:
What Reflection Do You See?

Questions for Thought and Reflection:

1. Is your testimony a reflection of who you say you are?

2. Or, does the reflection of your lifestyle make the evidence of your confession ineffective?

3. Who in your life has provided a reflection of Christ that has set an example for you, especially in challenging times? What was the impact of their reflection in your life?

Chapter 8

A Righteous Standard

For now, we see in a mirror dimly, but then face to face. Now I know in part; then I shall know fully, even as I have been fully known.
—1 CORINTHIANS 13:12

A Quagmire of Standards

MY HEALTH INSURANCE company has an office not far from where I live. While it is a sales office, they also offer free yoga classes three times a week to members. You can also stop in most any time during business hours and get a free check-up of blood pressure, blood sugar level, and cholesterol. It's awesome that I can just drop in most any time, and if the nurse is available, there is no waiting. There is also a machine that checks your weight, height, body mass index, and body fat composition. The device has been a bit perplexing to me. For the past month, each time it showed my height to be vastly different. It has fluctuated more than an inch in one direction or the other each time. With the erratic readings and inconsistencies, the machine is in obvious need of calibration. I stand as straight as I can because I actually want the machine to tell me that I am taller than I know I am. Like the Queen in the mirror, I admit that I would welcome hearing that I am perhaps two inches taller than I am. If I could do something to change my height, I'd increase it. But it is what it is, nonetheless. We have talked about my daughter who saw the mirrors not giving her the reflection she thought she should have. How reliable is the mirror to reflect the truth? Can the mirror lie?

Is it the mirror or is it simply our inability to see an accurate reflection? The Scripture says we see in the mirror dimly, implying that, for some reason, we do not see wholly or clearly from where we are today. Are we physically incapable of seeing our true reflection because of these earthly bodies? Or is it that we see dimly because we see through colored lenses, ingrained cultural factors, or even what other people have fed into our minds making us incapable of owning up to who or how we really are? Do we sometimes see only what we want to see because we imagine ourselves being a certain way, and we refuse to believe anything else? Do we rationalize and justify our behaviors and actions?

There are some who see themselves as good people—law-abiding, kind to others, givers, helpers in the community—and they are, but yet rationalize that they don't have to believe in God or accept Jesus Christ as Lord. I have heard comparisons to Christians: "I'm more kind or generous than they are, so how could God reject me?" Then there are the churchgoers who are faithful in their attendance and in giving tithes and offerings, but they are like the people described by the prophet Amos: performing the rituals and speaking the language but having no heart or zeal for God or love for other people.

I grew up with three sisters, who were at times brutally honest. We had not yet mastered the art of diplomacy or learned how to display attributes of compassion. We just "called it as we saw it," and that was that! If someone's attire was too revealing, our mother didn't have to correct us, because a sister (or several) would have the offender in check before our mother ever saw the attire. If I missed the bus or curfew, I don't know whose wrath I feared more, my dad's or my sisters'. If your boyfriend was thuggish, you would be sternly enlightened in case you tried to overlook those attributes or pretended like he was a gift from heaven. My upbringing was saturated with unbridled truth whether you wanted to hear it or not. The standards were set high, and there was an unwavering expectation of adherence. We didn't even recognize them as standards. There were no written rules, but you were nonetheless required to understand and walk accordingly.

The young men in the neighborhood where we grew up secretly referred to our house as "Fort Knox." My dad, a father of four beautiful daughters, also set high standards. His standards were not only set high, but they were also clearly known. The young men in the neighborhood knew that those standards existed and that they could not just freely come over to visit. There were a few who were either naïve and did not know or did not understand the gravity of his standards, or they carelessly put their life in their own hands and chose to test the rule. While the outcomes of such instances were embarrassing, to say the least, the young men left with a clear understanding of the seriousness of adhering to the standards. The young men did not have to be told twice.

While I had many good teachers and coaches, the great ones were those who forced me to take inventory of myself. Today, many have little to no understanding of the significance of having a measurable standard or perhaps any standards at all. The message is not just about having a standard. We could all have standards that are self-imposed, like those in my upbringing. We have differing beliefs and ideologies that we think are correct and thus define our standard and way of life. What then is the standard for a true reflection? Is there an example? Does the mirror lie? If we say that we are Christian, do we cast a reflection of Christ? What if we were each left to define our standards of living, like those who think that because they are kind, good, and giving, they don't need Christ?

A Moral Compass Needed

What may appear to be right to one person may be wrong for someone else. What may seem good to one may look evil to another. Just because a person has developed a set of standards that they hold high, why should others be required to follow those standards? We may have standards in our homes where we have authority to impose those standards. We have standards in the workplace where the employer has the authority to impose rules to ensure order. Even in the process of passing new laws, whether at the local, state, or federal level, there is a rigorous and arduous process that must be followed. We as citizens can even weigh in with our thoughts. But what happens when self-imposed standards are instituted? What makes that standard the model of what is right and good to be adhered to by all?

There have been widespread genocides because someone thought it was the right thing to do. There have been ethnic cleansings, where nations have been nearly wiped away just because someone thought one race of people was the only pure race and that all others should be extinguished. We continue to see such ideologies in play. We also see the effect of a lack of moral standards all around us in national, state, and local political agendas. We see it in our workplaces where decisions are sometimes made not for the good of the whole, but for the benefit of the privileged, or because it increases the bottom line regardless of its impact on people. We see it in our churches and homes, where individuals are left to their own devices doing what seems right and acceptable in their sight. According to Biblical Proverbs, "There is a way that seems right to a man." By natural perspectives, the matter may appear to be the right thing to do, but in the end, a different reality erupts.

In my earlier years as a development engineer working in quality control in the aerospace industry, we had standards. The standards were detailed and exact; they had been tested, tested, and tested again. The standards were precise—that is, there was no room for deviation, situational ethics, or personal interpretation. If the specs called for a part to be two inches in length, with a tolerance limit of plus or minus (+/-) .005, it was unacceptable if it measured outside the range of 1.995–2.005 inches, no matter how minute that deviation was. There were no exceptions. If it could not be reworked and brought into the predetermined and acceptable range, then it was rejected as scrap. Additionally, my responsibilities included testing select aircraft engine components to be sure that every batch of parts that came in continued to meet all of the required standards, including material properties, casting and manufacturing standards, machined specifications, as well as structural integrity. The parts could be tested without actually destroying them. You could not, however, just look at the external aspect of the parts and make a determination; they had to be evaluated under microscopic conditions and with specialized equipment to assess the unseen aspects to ensure compliance with design specifications and standards.

Likewise, we need a moral compass. We need a roadmap to serve as our standard and our guide in life. Psalm 37:23–24 says,

> *The steps of a good man are ordered by the LORD,*
> *And He delights in his way.*
> *Though he may fall, he shall not be utterly cast down;*
> *For the Lord upholds him with His hand (NKJV).*

The operative word here is good. A man may attempt to define what is good and resort to human reasoning. I have heard the expression numerous times concerning individuals: "She (or he) is a good person." While the term good is a common word with diverse meanings, it is best understood from a biblical perspective. Our human attempts to define good, fall short, and many have their unique interpretation of, or perspective on, good. If humankind were allowed to define good without basing it on a solid biblical foundation, there would be many different interpretations. It would lead to mass confusion and pandemonium in our society. We can describe someone as being a good person. That is fine, but subjective. What is good to one is not necessarily good to another. What then becomes our guide? What is our moral compass or roadmap? We could say that we do not need a guide or compass.

In a similar vein, I see beliefs that boundaries are not required to constrain us, that every person should be left to their knowledge, intellect, and creativity to do what they think is right. We can see similar kinds of subjectivity in the political realm of lawmaking. There is so much debate because there are many perspectives on right and wrong or what is and is not acceptable and permissible. The most recent US presidential election has set forth examples of how some of the nation's top leaders view right and wrong, moral or immoral. It is highly subjective, to say the least.

Scripture says that we are born with a sinful nature. That means that we have a natural predisposition or inclination toward sin. If humans are born with a disposition toward evil, then, left without a moral compass, it is evil that abounds. Corruption breeds corruption and becomes commonplace. The most absurd of beliefs become unbridled. Our environment today reminds me of television shows portraying the Wild, Wild West, where there were laws, but enforcement was left to the strongest and fastest gunslinger. Imagine if each person is left to set up personal standards without any retribution from the law—defining for oneself what is right and acceptable. Even our government recognizes the need for some level of uniformity and has set up laws and policies to guide society and provide a set of boundaries, though it appears from Internet blogs and chat rooms that the boundaries are growing wider and wider.

A few years ago, I relocated to south Florida. I found a beautiful condominium with breathtaking views, overlooking the intercoastal waterway. The process of securing the place, however, was somewhat alarming as there are so many lofty standards that tenants must comply with, including parking restrictions, garbage disposal, recycling rules and restrictions, and even being interviewed and approved for admittance by the community association's board of directors. But one of the most salient features that attracted me to the community was how immaculately and well-kept it was maintained. Its meticulous upkeep and well-manicured landscape, its mature foliage, with the waterfront views made it a difficult choice to pass up. But as I reflect on the high standards, it was no surprise that the community bode charm and sophistication while even some newer communities close by couldn't compare. The high standards it set, no doubt contributed to the longevity and aesthetic appeal of the community and will continue for years to come.

In contrast to another neighborhood where I once lived with my family: it, too, was an older, well-established community. While there was an active homeowners' association, the commitment to its standards seemed far less stringent. As an example, a neighbor parked his truck on the street in front of our house for almost six months; over time, debris collected around the tires. The owner never moved it, not once. Nor was it even cranked, as far as we could tell. Although the president of the neighborhood association filed a report, the traffic police patrolling the street, stopped and took note, but did nothing to rectify the situation. Nor did it appear that the police took action, even after the registration sticker expired. The truck sat there for at least another month. So, while standards existed within both communities, the care and consistency of commitment to those standards made a world of difference in the south Florida neighborhood.

If we confess to be Christian and commit to living a life representative of our confession, then we should ask: By what standards? Or whose standards? What is the standard that guides your moral viewpoint?

If we each could have a personal interpretation of what is right and acceptable, picking and choosing what Scripture passage to believe and what others to toss by the wayside, how would we differentiate ourselves in the world? There are some in the world who are kinder, and more pleasing to know and be around, than some who confess Christianity. The South Florida community held a high set of standards with which all residents and visitors were held accountable. The association's rules were firmly enforced. It seems that although the former community had restrictions and standards, they lacked commitment and effective enforcement. Over time, the beauty, aesthetic appeal, and sustainability of my previous neighborhood, which once boasted about its opulence and notable residents, eroded.

Only One Righteous Standard

The standard we seek is a righteous standard—an effective standard that is uniform and everlasting. It does not change over time or become outdated. It is not irrelevant, nor does it fluctuate based on the situation. In a righteous standard, there is no room for personal agendas, interpretations, or the vox populi. The righteous standard is designed to make our lives better than we could ever imagine or do for ourselves. It aims to lift us up, not to place additional weights upon us. It is a standard like at the South Florida community, which will yield significant benefits, but we must understand it and embrace it.

There is but one righteous standard established by the Lord God, our Creator, and it is personified in His Son Christ Jesus. There are some, like the disciple Thomas, who asked to see God. Jesus replied,

> *"If you had known me, you would have known my Father also. From now on you do know him and have seen him." Philip said*

> to him, "Lord, show us the Father, and it is enough for us." Jesus said to him, "Have I been with you so long, and you still do not know me, Philip? Whoever has seen me has seen the Father" (John 14:7–9).

If we profess to be Christian, we are to reflect a likeness of Jesus Christ. The very term Christian denotes "Christ-like." Dictionary.com describes the term Christian as pertaining to, believing in, or belonging to the religion based on the teachings of Jesus Christ. It is a person who exemplifies in his or her life the teachings of Christ, exhibiting a spirit proper to a follower of Jesus Christ.[25] The etymology of the term Christ indicates that it is a title given to Jesus of Nazareth, whose Hebrew name is Yeshua. The Old English word Crist originated from the Latin name Christus, from the Greek word Khristos, meaning "the anointed." The Hebrew word is Mashiah or, as we know it, Messiah, meaning "to rub or anoint." Messiah translated into English also means "anointed one," so it was translated into old Greek as Khristos and later in English as Christ.

The word Christian was a name given by the Romans to the followers of Jesus. The disciples were first called "Christians" at Antioch (Acts 11:26), about A.D. 43. They, however, were among themselves called, brethren (Acts 15:1, 23; 1 Corinthians 7:12), disciples (Acts 9:26; 11:29), believers (Acts 5:14), and saints (Romans 8:27; 15:25).[26]

While we may see standards as a simple set of guiding principles or rules, we have the Holy Scriptures—as the inspired and anointed teachings of God that provide light, hope, redemption, and direction. Second Timothy 3:16 says, "All Scripture is breathed out by God and profitable for teaching, for reproof, for correction, and for training in righteousness." Every passage in the biblical text is inspired by God, with a man serving as a scribe. All Scripture is useful in working to bring about

---

25 http://www.dictionary.com/browse/christian?s=t
26 M. G. Easton, *Illustrated Bible Dictionary,* 3rd ed. (New York: Thomas Nelson, 1897), at http://www.biblestudytools.com/dictionaries/eastons-bible-dictionary/christian.html.

transformation in our lives when we follow it. God is constantly speaking, leading, and guiding. However, we are many times incapable of seeing or hearing because He gets drowned out by all of the clutter in our lives. While the Bible, His Holy Word, is our guide, compass, and roadmap for life, its author is the only righteous standard.

In 2 Corinthians, the apostle Paul discusses how "the natural man" is incapable of understanding God's revelations, including His written Word, spiritual gifts, the divine nature of God, or Jesus Christ, the Son of God. While professing Christianity, such people walk with veiled faces incapable of seeing divine revelation or understanding. Many books that line shelves and so much material available on the Internet offer misleading interpretations that lead unsuspecting people away from the truths of God. As the Scripture says in 1 Corinthians 2:9–12:

> *"9 But, as it is written, "What no eye has seen, nor ear heard, nor the heart of man imagined, what God has prepared for those who love him"— 10 these things God has revealed to us through the Spirit. For the Spirit searches everything, even the depths of God.11 For who knows a person's thoughts except for the spirit of that person, which is in him? So also no one comprehends the thoughts of God except the Spirit of God.12 Now we have received not the spirit of the world, but the Spirit who is from God, that we might understand the things freely given us by God."*

Further, Paul underscores this point in verses 14–16:

> *"14 The natural person does not accept the things of the Spirit of God, for they are folly to him, and he is not able to understand them because they are spiritually discerned. 15 The spiritual person judges all things but is himself to be judged by no one. 16 "For who has understood the mind of the Lord so as to instruct him?" But we have the mind of Christ."*

A Righteous Standard

Humans have contrived many laws, philosophies, ideologies, and diverse beliefs and opinions out of natural understanding. There are many perspectives and schools of thought. The natural mind is incapable of understanding transcendent revelation. Even if these are contrived with all sincerity and deep-seated beliefs within a person's heart, a transcendent perspective of holiness and righteousness can be manifested and understood only through the presence and work of the Holy Spirit.

All things are made possible by our Lord and Creator through His Son, the Holy Spirit, and the biblical text. The bottom line is that there is only one Righteous Standard of our God, revealed through the life, character, and nature of Christ Jesus. There is no other, nor is there anything that can usurp his authority and the supremacy of his existence. Hebrews 1:1–3 makes clear that;

> *"Long ago, at many times and in many ways, God spoke to our fathers by the prophets, but in these last days, he has spoken to us by his Son, whom he appointed the heir of all things, through whom also he created the world. He is the radiance of the glory of God and the exact imprint of his nature, and he upholds the universe by the word of his power. After making purification for sins, he sat down at the right hand of the Majesty on high, having become as much superior to angels as the name he has inherited is more excellent than theirs."*

God has given us Jesus Christ as the Righteous Standard. We are to always stand for what is right in the sight of the Lord, but we can do so only by the power and presence of the Holy Spirit in our lives. Your life may be that glimpse of Christ to inspire others to seek more transcendent revelation.

Mirror, Mirror:
What Reflection Do You See?

Questions for Thought and Reflection:

1. What standards have you been expected to adhere to and how were they aligned with the Biblical teachings?

2. What standards have you imposed deliberately or unintended on others and in what ways did those standards influence them?

Chapter 9

To Mirror God Is to Know God

Therefore, be imitators of God, as beloved children. And walk in love, as Christ loved us and gave himself up for us, a fragrant offering and sacrifice to God. Ephesians 5:1

Imitation or Pretense

WHILE MANY OF the epistles of Paul forewarn believers and new converts to Christ about false doctrines and false prophets who are like wolves wearing sheep's clothing, pretending and putting on a pretense, he also encourages imitation. From a biblical perspective, imitation is what Paul advocates, telling his listeners to follow him as he follows Christ. The very thought of imitating someone else regardless of who they are has become taboo in our modern day. People have been criticized and mocked for trying to imitate someone else. The media are always on watch and regularly commenting on who is trying to imitate who in style or dress or behavior. By the world's standards, it just isn't fashionable to imitate others. They are seen as copycats or people who have no vision or fresh ideas of their own. Additionally, we see the fake-it-till-you-make-it attitude, which has also received its share of criticism. Both notions of, imitation, and "fake it till you make it" are thought to be matters of pretense.

But aren't these presuppositions more like double-sided coins? On the one side, the worldly perspectives appear to be like dressed-up deception. Paul warns us about these false prophets. This side of the coin questions a person's motives, character, and self-centered actions to achieve for oneself. These are individuals who act with pretense, are impure in their motives, and have no desire for God in their hearts. We can put on an act of kindness or love for a while, but if our hearts are far from it, it is only a matter of time before the truth is revealed. We can smile and be pleasant on the outside, while inside filled with disdain, deception, or even indifference, having no thought or concern whatsoever toward another.

On the other side of the coin, however, is genuinely striving toward something by imitating and practicing the behaviors and attributes modeled by Christ or a disciple of Christ until those practices become a natural part of who we are. It is imitation driven by a desire to improve in some area of life or to become a better person in some way. In a prior chapter, we talked about the effects of mirroring. We can see how babies mimic or imitate what they see and hear. Sometimes it is so cute how they can repeat something they heard, without any understanding of its meaning. They regurgitate it at just the right moment. They also act out motions and emotions that they have seen. They are imitating what they saw or heard. While I consider myself to be an individualist, always having new ideas and vision, and purpose, I can think of many people throughout my life that have made positive and influential contributions, and many of them have no knowledge of just how much. I have imitated some attributes and characteristics and adopted them into my behaviors to improve who I am and how I am. One such person is a former supervisor who had a very impressive vocabulary.

Whenever I was in his presence, and he used a word unfamiliar to me, I would write it down, secretly, and look it up later. I never admitted that I didn't know what a word meant. I pretended to know. Because he challenged me, my vocabulary multiplied in a short period. Without seeing our reflection, how will we know where we need to improve? Without a deliberate action plan, improvement may be stalled. It's also a reminder of a familiar scripture that without a vision, we perish.

Many translations use the word imitate, as Paul is instructing the early church to imitate him as he imitates Christ. The opening verse from Ephesians 5 teaches us to imitate Christ. The word "imitate" however, is not just to mimic without heart or purpose. Nor does it mean that we are pretentious. The word means to "replicate" or "reproduce." Genesis 1:25 talks about reproducing after one's own kind. So, as Christians, we too need a model, an example, and we are encouraged to reproduce after the example, provided for us. Our example is Jesus Christ.

Jeremiah 17:9 says, "The heart is deceitful above all things, and desperately wicked, who can understand it?" Jesus addresses this in Mark 7:21–22: "For from within, out of the heart of man, come evil thoughts, sexual immorality, theft, murder, adultery, coveting, wickedness, deceit, sensuality, envy, slander, pride, foolishness. All these evil things come from within, and they defile a person." There is no emphasis on the external. It is an inner work that is manifested externally, whether we know it or not. Paul's instruction of imitating Christ is more about practicing and emulating godly character and attributes than being pretentious about the external. Paul's teaching is particularly useful if our hearts lack a desire to personify godly character and qualities.

Beyond Imitation

Mirroring God entails more than imitation. Simply speaking, to mirror God is to know God. To know God encompasses a great deal more. God is all-powerful and all knowing. He is omnipotent, omniscient, and omnipresent. God is the self-existent One, the Alpha and the Omega, the Beginning and the End. He shall rule and reign from everlasting to everlasting. He is the hope of our salvation, a lamp unto our feet, a light unto our path. God is everything we need and so much more. A foundational question is; do we know God? Do we have a relationship with God?

In some theological studies, a question raised is, "Why do only a small percentage of those converting to Christianity fail to remain faithful to their confession?"[27] The world is looking and judging. They silently observe one's character and behavior to see if the righteous standard of God is displayed and the teachings of Christ Jesus are evident. If we know that the standard is Christ and that we are called to bear witness of Christ in our lives, there must be more than a casual acquaintance before He can be emulated.

While there are arranged marriages in some countries, as is their custom, here in the United States it is customary that when you meet someone and seriously consider marriage, you spend time getting to know that person. It is just the opposite with Christ: we must come to accept Him by faith first and receive the baptism of the Holy Spirit. There is no other way. We chose to believe and accept, or we don't. While there may arguably be gray areas in life, there is no gray area here. It is yes or no, do or don't, black or white, no gray. The question of whether we accept Christ as Lord of our life demands a response.

It is then through the Holy Spirit that we can come to understand the precepts and teachings of Christ. The good news is that, unlike the world's standards, where we spend so much time trying to adorn ourselves and put forth our best when dating someone or perhaps when applying for a new position, Christ says to "come as you are." We don't

---

27 Charles Finney, *Finney's Systematic Theology*, ed. Dennis Carrol, Bill Nicely, and L.G. Parkhurst, Jr. (Minneapolis,
　MN: Bethany House, 1994), xiii.

have to put on airs. We don't have to go and buy new outfits or learn to play golf or tennis or learn another language just to impress or keep up. We don't even have to make excuses for our fleshly habits and desires because he already knows that we were born with a sin nature. He is the one who made a way for us to receive a new life. Just think, we simply come as we are, with a sincere desire to make Him the Lord of our life and receive His great gift of salvation provided for us. The Lord our God already knows us better than we know ourselves. He sees the innermost parts of us, including things that we don't yet see or know about ourselves. Though we may not know all there is to know about God, He knows everything about us.

The apostle Paul affirms that those attempting to understand Scripture or spiritual things cannot do so with the natural mind. Again, he points out that transcendent matters are like foolishness to the natural mind; they must be spiritually discerned and understood (1 Corinthians 2:14). It explains why the world is baffled by the supernatural manifestations of God and mock what they see. As Paul expounds, it is impossible for the natural man to understand the spiritual things, for they are foolishness to someone for whom a spiritual transformation has not yet taken place. They are hidden from the natural mind no matter how intelligent one may believe him, or herself to be. There is a God-ordained process; one must first believe and accept Christ Jesus as Lord and Savior to receive the gift of the Holy Spirit, thereby, enabling us to understand the things of God.

It is only after exercising our faith to receive Christ Jesus as our Lord and Savior that we are better equipped to see and spiritually understand the precepts of God and develop a spiritual and intimate relationship with God. It is impossible to see or know without having a spiritual connection with Jesus Christ as Lord and Savior and the baptism of the Holy Spirit to bring total enlightenment. It is not a one-time experience but a continual process. It is a lifetime journey. As 1

Corinthians 13:12 states, we see only in part today the magnificence of God. As we continue to grow in the grace and knowledge of God, we see so much more of who He is and how awesome He is. We have oneness with Him. For me, this has been the journey of my life. I wouldn't want it any other way.

Scripture provides an ethical standard that surpasses worldly expectations of ordinary men and women. It calls us to a morality that exceeds our own measure or standard of righteousness. When we look at matters of imitation, it depends on who or what is being imitated. We are biblically instructed not to copy the behavior and customs of this world, but to let God transform us into a new person (Romans 12:2). Though we can describe the nature, the attributes, and the character of God, it would be erroneous to think that any of us could incorporate these into our lives completely on our own. It doesn't work that way. We are not capable of transforming ourselves, even with the numerous self-help books and videos available in the marketplace today. Yes, we do have a part, and we can even make some progress. But getting to the root cause, to bring complete freedom and victory, requires more than our human capability.

We must personally submit to the will of God and allow the Holy Spirit to work in us. If we attempt to transform on our own, we may rationalize or justify why some things should remain as they are. These may be the areas God wants to transform first and foremost. When we think that we can transform on our own, it opens up the probability of compromise. We may have memories that are so painful, or ugly, that we want to pretend they never existed. Those too are things that God wants to reveal and dig up. Those are areas that God wants to bring healing, forgiveness, or deliverance. Further, we may selectively hold on to certain beliefs and ideologies because they sound good or are so popularly acceptable. If everybody else is doing it and they are prospering, we may think that it must be okay. Sometimes, we may even believe that some of these ideologies are scriptural. How many times have you heard someone ask, "Isn't that in the Bible?" If we think that we can transform ourselves, we then take on the notion that we do not need God—that we can do these things on our own. The words of my firstborn daughter still ring in my memory as it appeared to be her favorite sentence: "I can do it myself." It wasn't just a statement for her; it was a bold declaration to tell me, her mother, to get out of the way or don't do anything to help—because she didn't need help. While it's cute to see a toddler take on such independence, it is another matter when it becomes a way of life for an adult. It can evolve into a form of pride. Its deceptive underpinnings can cause us to distance ourselves from God and circumvent the transformative process and a real relationship with God.

There are things about us or within us that we may not recognize or see clearly in the mirror. But God does, and He wants to clean it away. Sometimes I go to the far depths of my closet looking for a particular garment, and in the process, I find other clothes that I have overlooked for years. I had forgotten about those garments. I'm elated to find them so that I can wear them and put them to good use. Likewise, there are things in my spiritual closet that God continues to bring to light, even after many years of going through a transformational process. As we commit to living in obedience to God's Word, we are continually being transformed and increasingly conformed into the image and likeness of Christ Jesus. While there may be some behaviors that are changed miraculously in an instant, others may take years of faithful obedience or even professional, biblically based counseling and prayers of deliverance. I have heard many testimonies from people who struggled for years to quit some habitual vice. When they committed themselves to the Lord, suddenly they lost their unsavory desire. They stopped smoking and never went back, or they have been fully delivered from some vice when nothing else had worked before. There are others who did not receive instant deliverance but remained committed to Christ and over time were healed and delivered. If we have committed ourselves to Christ, then we have also committed to being Christ-like—that is, to take on His nature, character, and moral attributes. 1 Peter 1:14–16 says, "As obedient children, do not be conformed to the passions of your former ignorance, but as he who called you is holy, you also be holy in all your conduct, since it is written, 'You shall be holy, for I am holy.'"

Knowing God

Many of us are acquainted with the Ten Commandments given by the Lord to Moses at Mount Sinai. We see them as a standard of behavior. While they indeed are, they alone do not provide a full understanding who God is and ensure us of a personal relationship with the God we serve.

An essential first step in building a relationship with our Lord is to study the Holy Scriptures of God. We are implored to go beyond merely reading. We are to study the Word and show ourselves approved (2 Timothy 2:15). Nor is it enough to go to church religiously but then never take time to read, pray, or study the Bible. God has given us His word, the Holy Scriptures as a roadmap for life. The Bible is where we find knowledge, wisdom, and illumination. It is a tool that arms us while we dwell in the midst of a cosmic war zone. Scripture makes clear that there is one, the devil, who goes around like a roaring lion and seeks to devour whomever it can (1 Peter 5:8). The Bible equips us; it provides examples of how to be and how not to be. It provides insights concerning our purpose for existence and our future. Further, scripture reveals the character and nature of God and how we are to live in a relationship with God. One example among many from the word of God is Psalm 119:9–16. It provides some insight regarding the statutes of the Lord. Try reading it out loud.

How can a young man keep his way pure?
By guarding it according to your Word.

With my whole heart I seek you;
let me not wander from your commandments!
I have stored up your word in my heart,
that I might not sin against you.
Blessed are you, O LORD;
teach me your statutes!
With my lips I declare
all the rules of your mouth.
In the way of your testimonies I delight
as much as in all riches.
I will meditate on your precepts
and fix my eyes on your ways.
I will delight in your statutes;
I will not forget your word.

I heard a story of someone named in the will of a very wealthy distant relative. Upon notice, the beneficiary immediately read the will from beginning to end, not taking any time for meals or breaks. The beneficiary was so excited about the treasure that had been left by this wealthy relative whom he hardly knew. The relative, however, knew a lot about the beneficiary, as expressed in the document with much love, care, and concern—and bequeathing a treasure chest. Metaphorically speaking, this is like the Holy Scriptures that God has given to us—to reveal His love, care, and concern for us. It is filled with and leads us to treasures and all that we need to be blessed and prosperous. But, we must take time to explore all that He has provisioned as detailed throughout Scripture.

It is not enough to be knowledgeable. To be knowledgeable but not obedient to what we know, is comparable to those who can quote or hypothesize the Word but live without any relationship with God. There is a call to obedience in the things that we know. It is a commitment to obedience in every aspect, without picking and choosing only those things that make us feel good or fit into our lifestyle. If we rationalize and justify our sin, then it makes us a sinner. But if we face truth and confess our sins, the Father is faithful and just to forgive us for our sin and unrighteousness. We are free.

Transformation comes by actual submission. True submission is exemplified through persistent obedience. It is also a process whereby we accept knowledge and revelation of our behaviors and characteristics that are misaligned with God's will and sometimes without understanding. It is acknowledging the truth about what is revealed and embracing change where needed. Isaiah 28:10 describes an applicable process: "For it is precept upon precept, precept upon precept, line upon line, line upon line, here a little, there a little."

Additional insights are found in 1 John 2:2-6. The New King James Bible translates it in this way:

> "*2 And He Himself is the propitiation for our sins, and not for ours only but also for the whole world. 3 Now by this we know that we know Him, if we keep His commandments. 4 He who says, "I know Him," and does not keep His commandments, is a liar, and the truth is not in him. 5 But whoever keeps His word, truly the love of God is perfected in him. By this we know that we are in Him. 6 He who says he abides in Him ought himself also to walk just as He walked." (NKJV)*

It is continual submission and obedience that leads to a transformed life. Our role in the transformative process is submission and obedience. It is unlike surgery, where we are anesthetized and while deep asleep the doctor performs all of the work, and when we are awakened, everything is done. Our relationship with God and the transformational process requires our full participation. The more we draw close to God, the more he draws near to us (James 4:8). And Psalm 119:1–6 states:

Blessed are those whose way is blameless,
 who walk in the law of the Lord!
Blessed are those who keep his testimonies,
 who seek him with their whole heart,
who also do no wrong,
 but walk in his ways!
You have commanded your precepts
 to be kept diligently.
Oh that my ways may be steadfast
 in keeping your statutes!
Then I shall not be put to shame,
 having my eyes fixed on all your commandments.

A lot can be said about obedience. The central point about transformation and a core message of this book is obedience. Think about the multitudes who profess to be Christians but live a life that is far from any resemblance of Christ-like living. Luke 16:10 says that the "one who is faithful in a very little is also faithful in much, and one who is dishonest in a very little is also dishonest in much." God wants to lavish us with good gifts—but not only material things. We must be in a place to receive them if we are to understand and know the value of the gift fully. It might be considered a bit artless to tell someone how much a gift is worth, or what you paid for it. But you might be very upset if you paid thousands of dollars for a rare painting or a piece of jewelry, and the recipient treated it as if it came from the five-and-dime store because he or she did not understand its full value.

God has given us a gift of His Son, Jesus, but do we understand the value of this priceless gift? In its simplest form, it boils down to the belief that He is the Son of God made manifest in the flesh. It is also an acknowledgment of the necessity of commitment and obedience as being the actions that demonstrate our belief. There are those who choose to follow the teachings of Christ, and there are those who decide to profess and live otherwise. When we are fully committed, we are faithful, unswerving, and steadfast (1 Corinthians 15:58). Transformation does not take place without a willing participant.

The root word of obedience is "obey," which comes from the Greek hupakou. It means to "hear" or "listen attentively"; by implication, it means to "heed" or "conform to a command or authority." It emphasizes an action of faithfully following authority and instructions. It is not contingent upon situations as some have questioned. There is no choice or personal interpretation regarding the matter. It is simply obedience to all of God's commands, whether one agrees or not. Deuteronomy 6:4–9 says:

> *"You shall love the LORD your God with all your heart and with all your soul and with all your might. And these words that I command you today shall be in your heart. You shall teach them diligently to your children and shall talk of them when you sit in your house, and when you walk by the way, and when you lie down, and when you rise. You shall bind them as a sign on your hand, and they shall be as frontlets between your eyes. You shall write them on the doorposts of your house and on your gates."*

Love is a core attribute of the nature of God. We are entreated to love God and to do likewise in our relationships with others. It is not a choice, but a charge. "Beloved, let us love one another, for love is from God, and whoever loves has been born of God and knows God. Anyone who does not love does not know God, because God is love…Beloved, if God so loved us, we also ought to love one another" (1 John 4:7–8, 11). When I think about God and all that I have come to understand about God, if I had to choose one word to describe God, it would be love.

All that He is and all that he is capable of doing is embodied and personified in the notion of love. It is much more than what is represented by the media and entertainment industry of today. Love is much more than those emotional roller-coaster rides of puppy-love experiences during our adolescent years. It is much more than what we might think about when we consider all that our parents or grandparents have done for us to make our lives better than theirs. Love is so much more than what we might have experienced or can imagine with the best of friends, even those who never exposed any secrets or embarrassing moments. Love is much more than merely reciting the words to others without demonstration. It is more than speaking words from a place of emptiness within, because you seek to win brownie points or score some victory. So "what is love?" you might ask.

If the Scripture says that God is love, then it must be an attribute present in the life of every believer. Love is a concept that is deeply rooted in the biblical text and Christian traditions. There are four types of love commonly described in the Greek language—Storge, Philia, Eros, and Agape—and three of these are discussed in the New Testament. It is important to understand how they are each distinctly different and each represents a particular type of love.

Storge is a natural affection that occurs within the family structure, like that felt by parents toward their children or between siblings and other extended members of the family. Romans 12:9–10 has often been referred to as the identifying mark of a true believer's life. It stresses to "let love be genuine. Abhor what is evil; hold fast to what is good. Love one another with brotherly affection." The apostle Paul goes on to illustrate the concept of brotherly love. In verses 10–13, he exhorts us to "outdo one another in showing honor. Do not be slothful in zeal, be fervent in spirit, serve the Lord. Rejoice in hope, be patient in tribulation, be constant in prayer. Contribute to the needs of the saints and seek to show hospitality."

Philia love is described as friendship or tender affection. It is a love that may include loyalty to friends, family, and community, and requires virtue, equality, and familiarity.

Eros love is an erotic or passionate love, from which English derives the word erotic. It denotes intimacy but does not have to be sexual. It is not used in the New Testament or Greek Old Testament (Septuagint), but I would say that this is the kind of love described in the Song of Solomon, though some theologians ascribe it as being a depiction of God's love toward His people.

Agape love is the form of love that is most associated with God's love toward humanity. Believers experience an extraordinary, and unconditional love of God. Agape is used interchangeably with Phileo to designate God the Father's love for Jesus (John 3:35), God the Father's love for an individual believer (John 14:21), and of Christ's love for a disciple (John 13:23)."[28] Agape love is the essence of who God is. Agape love is the most powerful example of our relationship with God and a demonstration of the nature of God. It is refreshing and compelling to know that God's love toward humankind is not based on "good works" or best behavior. His love is not based on an emotional experience or evanescent feelings. It is His will. He loves unconditionally. It is a choice, and we, too, are called to choose to love, unconditionally. I liken it to parenting children. I love and have always loved my daughters. Even when they did things that caused me great disappointment, I still loved them. I just didn't always love or even like some of the misbehavior. When others revile, persecute us, mistreat us, it is agape love that enables us to demonstrate the character and nature of God. As the Scripture instructs,

> *"Love your enemies and pray for those who persecute you, so that you may be sons of your Father who is in heaven. For he makes his sun rise on the evil and on the good and sends rain on the just and on the unjust. For if you love those who love you, what reward do you have? Do not even the tax collectors do the same? And if you greet only your brothers, what more are you doing than others? Do*

---

28 Chad Brand, gen. ed., *Holman Illustrated Bible Dictionary,* rev. ed. (Nashville: Holman Reference, 2015), s.v. "love."

not even the Gentiles do the same? You, therefore, must be perfect, as your heavenly Father is perfect" (Matthew 5:44–48).

We are differentiated as disciples of Christ when we show love to those who despise us, persecute us, mistreat us, or gossip about us, or worse. We achieve a different set of results when we pray regarding the matter and the person.

There are occasions and encounters where love for others is not easily done, but it can be done. I once worked for an organization that attempted to make the workforce much more pleasing and collegial. The company wanted to encourage respect, harmony, and team spirit within the workplace and, therefore, instituted a set of guiding principles. They created banners for the hallways and break rooms, to remind employees of these principles. One of the large banners hung on the wall just outside my office. So, among all of the principles, this is the one I remember the most—to this day: "Think the Best About Others First." It is a powerful statement; of all places, where would we be most challenged in thinking the best about others? In the workplace, where we depend on other people to help us complete projects and meet deadlines. If they fail, what thoughts do we internalize? Yes, we may have a conversation with them, but what thoughts linger? Does our trust and confidence in others fall precipitously? I have worked with too many people who blatantly held the attitude, "just do it and beg forgiveness later," knowing full well from the beginning that they were skating on thin ice. We can also think about how we might feel when something happens, and others form opinions of us without having the full details. Our thoughts about others can impede the transformational process. Romans 12:2 says that we are transformed by the renewing our minds. Our thought life has a tremendous impact on our behaviors and attitudes. We must allow our thinking to consider grounds for a sound explanation. Condemning and demoralizing a person before gathering all information is not something that you would welcome for your own life. It's not something you should lay on others. I think about the people in my life who had little knowledge about me. They were so thoughtful and talked about the good things and the accomplishments and exercised hospitality and exhortation. They could have chosen to speak about the blunders and the mistakes I've made and decided not to build a relationship. It is refreshing when we choose to build up rather than tear down.

Agape love involves making a conscious decision. One of my favorite narratives concerning the attribute of love is in the New Testament, 1 Corinthians 13. It tells us what love is and what it isn't. The Message Bible conveys it this way:

> *"If I speak with human eloquence and angelic ecstasy but don't love, I'm nothing but the creaking of a rusty gate.*
>
> *If I speak God's Word with power, revealing all his mysteries and making everything plain as day, and if I have faith that says to a mountain, "Jump," and it jumps, but I don't love, I'm nothing.*
>
> *If I give everything I own to the poor and even go to the stake to be burned as a martyr, but I don't love, I've gotten nowhere. So, no matter what I say, what I believe, and what I do, I'm bankrupt without love.*
>
> *Love never gives up.*
> *Love cares more for others than for self.*
> *Love doesn't want what it doesn't have.*
> *Love doesn't strut,*
> *Doesn't have a swelled head,*
> *Doesn't force itself on others,*
> *Isn't always "me first,"*
> *Doesn't fly off the handle,*
> *Doesn't keep score of the sins of others,*
> *Doesn't revel when others grovel,*
> *Takes pleasure in the flowering of truth,*

Puts up with anything,
Trusts God always,
Always looks for the best,
Never looks back,
But keeps going to the end.

Love never dies. Inspired speech will be over some day; praying in tongues will end; understanding will reach its limit. We know only a portion of the truth, and what we say about God is always incomplete. But when the Complete arrives, our incompletes will be canceled.

When I was an infant at my mother's breast, I gurgled and cooed like any infant. When I grew up, I left those infant ways for good.

We don't yet see things clearly. We're squinting in a fog, peering through a mist. But it won't be long before the weather clears and the sun shines bright! We'll see it all then, see it all as clearly as God sees us, knowing him directly just as he knows us!

But for right now, until that completeness, we have three things to do to lead us toward that consummation: Trust steadily in God, hope unswervingly, love extravagantly. And the best of the three is love."

Love trumps greed and selfishness. Just think what might happen in our lives and communities if we could make our number one focus to love the Lord God with all of our mind, soul, and spirit and to love others in this same way just as Christ loves the church. How much of the world's evil could be eradicated? How could much more peace be ushered in? Many of the evils of the world—especially wars and conflict among nations—emanate from greed. It is a desire to be the biggest, the most privileged, and the dominant power, even at the expense of others. The quotation "All is fair in love and war" restated in a biblical worldview would read, "Where love abounds, peace abounds all the more."

Mirror, Mirror:
What Reflection Do You See?

Questions for Thought and Reflection:

1. Do you know God? In what ways do you know God?

2. In what ways do you cast a reflection of God?

3. Of those cited herein, what would you say are your strongest areas in knowing God: Study of Scripture, Prayer, Submission/Obedience, Love?

4. What other ways can you think of that enables us in growing our relationship with God?

Chapter 10

A Righteous Reflection

A FEW YEARS AGO, I attended the Miss Black USA Pageant in Washington, DC. I vividly recall the liturgical dance performed by a contestant who was ultimately crowned Miss Black USA. There was something very hallowed about her expression through dance, and it seemed as if she was dancing out her testimony of the presence and power of God in her life. I apparently wasn't the only one who felt so. The mistress of ceremonies later commented that it felt as if the contestant had just preached a sermon without ever speaking a word. I think this is a good analogy, exemplary of how we are to live as disciples of Christ every day. Not the dancing per se, but our being a living testimony of Christ Jesus, even without speaking a word. It was a genuine inner reflection that shined outwardly.

We are constantly being observed even when we least expect. Have you ever gotten an unexpected job offer from another company or division within a company, or an unexpected promotion? Imagine that someone just approached you and said, "We think you are perfect for this position." You were being observed. It has happened to me a few times over the course of my career and it is certainly better than trying to convince someone in an interview why I should be hired. Perhaps that's the advantage of being observed.

If we could never utter a word, our lifestyle, our character, our ethics, and our moral behavior should emulate and reflect Jesus Christ within us. There are some who only observe us. They may never hear a word we speak. We can impact many lives every day. What reflection do they see? There are far too many who are called "Christians" who cast a reflection that is not appreciably different from the reflection cast by non-Christians. Their values are aligned with the world. They have little knowledge and understanding of God's Word. On the other end of the spectrum, we know that holistically, as disciples, we are witnesses for Christ. That is, our lives, reflected through our lifestyles, our values, moral aptitude, words, conversation, and speech are all to be a reflection of Christ Jesus. Our testimony is not always verbal or oral. Our presence alone speaks of Christ Jesus.

You Too Are a Mirror for Others

While we have focused a lot on our inner being and how it might compare or align with godly principles and teachings, there is also another aspect of the transformation process, and that is how others see us. Do we give enough attention to how others view us, or do we even care? As a young engineer working in a male-dominated manufacturing environment for a major automotive company, my manager perceived me as being "unapproachable." I failed to understand how this was my problem. It seemed to be the other person's problem if he felt that he could not approach me." My manager disagreed! I had responsibility for overseeing the quality of the engine components being manufactured, machined, and tested before their assembly and shipment. If there was a problem in that process, I was the assigned engineer that others had to seek out for resolution. But for some unknown reason, they felt they could not approach me. Could it be that these men were intimidated by my size at five feet three inches tall and 105 pounds? My attitude was that they needed to follow the written procedures, regardless of how they felt.

I now see that there were perhaps many perspectives on this issue that could have been argued, debated, or questioned. There are also perhaps many views on the matter of what reflection others see in us. Some Christians take an attitude similar to the opinion I had thirty years ago—that they do not live their lives to please others. Some take the perspective that nobody is going to like them anyway, so why should they waste their time trying to please others? Then some feel that there are people who will always find something to criticize, no matter how righteous one may live or try to live. No one is perfect. To some degree, these are all true. It is not about doing things to please others as it is about being disciples of Christ. We are instructed to live righteous and holy lives before God. Scripture also indicates that secular onlookers should be able to see us as being set apart from the world. How is it then that they will know who the disciples of Christ are? Will they be able to pick you or me out of a crowd? Do they recognize us as such in the workplace? How will they know?

There is an evident outward manifestation of the inner workings of the Holy Spirit. It begins with a yielded and submissive Spirit that believers possess when allowing the Holy Spirit to work in one's heart, soul, and mind. A Christian reflection is exemplified by virtues taught in God's Word. How does Christ distinguish His true servants from those who are still of this world? Jesus taught in the Sermon on the Mount: "You will recognize them by their fruits. Are grapes gathered from thorn bushes or figs from thistles? So, every healthy tree bears good fruit, but the diseased tree bears bad fruit" (Matthew 7:16–17). This Scripture says that those who profess to be disciples of Christ shall cast a reflection and that they shall be known according to the fruit they bear. The silent testimony of the Christian life is equally or more important than talking about who you are and what you believe. We may never have an opportunity to speak a word to them verbally, but we communicate through the testimony of our faith by the fruit we bear. A person's outer behavior is often an indication of one's inner make-up. Conversely, when an internal conflict exists, it can also be exhibited in external actions.

Paul's letter to the Galatians speaks of the works of the flesh and describes those with a sinful and unregenerate nature. Galatians then describes the fruit of the Spirit, which makes evident the character, nature, and transformation of those who are submitted to the will of God. Paul is precise about what this fruit consists of and what we see in the transformed life. "The Fruit of the Spirit is love, joy, peace, patience, kindness, goodness, faithfulness, gentleness, and self-control… Those who belong to Christ Jesus have crucified the flesh with its passions and desires" (Galatians 5:22–23).

Such are the many aspects of the "fruit," which is singular, denoting that while it may have many facets, it has one result: fruit. As listed in Galatians 5, the fruit of the Spirit is simply a reflection of God's character reproduced in us by His Spirit. While Galatians 5 is widely known for its discourse and teachings on the "fruit" of the Spirit, it is not a subject that is restricted only to Galatians 5. The term fruit is embodied throughout all of Scripture and is used approximately 253 times throughout the King James translation, from Genesis to Revelation. There are many definitions of the word fruit, and approximately forty-three are cited in Strong's Concordance. Further, Dictionary.com defines fruit as anything produced, or accruing, a product, result, or effect; return or profit. What fruit should God's Spirit produce in us?

The word "fruit" is used throughout Scripture and is used both in a literal and figurative sense. A few examples of its use include fruit as produce that yields something, as in Genesis 1:12 (NIV): "The land produced vegetation: plants bearing seed according to their kinds and trees bearing fruit with seed in it according to their kind." It is further used in Genesis 1:22, to denote fish, fowl, and animal offspring. "And God blessed them, saying, 'Be fruitful and multiply and fill the waters in the seas, and let birds multiply on the earth." In Deuteronomy 28:4 (NIV), fruit is about agriculture and livestock, and the fertility of a woman. "The fruit of your womb will be blessed, and the crops of your land and the young of your livestock — the calves of your herds and the lambs of your flocks."

The term fruit is also used metaphorically to describe one's character, nature, and behavioral attributes, as seen in Proverbs 1:31: "They shall eat the fruit of their way, and have their fill of their own devices." It speaks to those who commit ungodly works—whatever things they do shall come back upon them. Hosea 10:13 speaks of "fruit" as the consequence of one's actions,

> *You have plowed iniquity;*
> *you have reaped injustice;*
> *you have eaten the* fruit *of lies.*
> *Because you have trusted in your own way*
> *and in the multitude of your warriors,*

A common theme regarding fruit is that it is seen as the result of one's actions. It is the evidence of what we are. John 15:2 validates that our Christian walk is progressive. Jesus likens Himself to a vine and the Lord God as a vinedresser and asserts that "every branch in me that does not bear fruit he takes away, and every branch that does bear fruit he prunes, that it may bear more fruit." The Lord God takes from us those parts of us that are contrary to His image—our weaknesses and vices that deter us from spiritual growth. Godly attributes are pruned to make them even more productive and vivid. Sometimes we might think that we are experiencing challenges in life because we lack in faith, holiness, or spiritual maturity. In fact, it may be just the opposite, that God wants to magnify and grow that part of us that is producing good fruit.

Galatians 5 refers to one's character, behavior, one's speech or thoughts. It refers to "fruit" as "wisdom." The fruit is a mirror or a mechanism that provide insights to one's inner being—a window to the soul. Fruit is the outward manifestation of what's inside of us. Like a tree, when it's watered and nourished from within, it produces fruit on the outside. We don't see the nourishment or change taking place inside the tree, but we know from its external appearance if it is nourished or malnourished. Although I lived on a farm with my grandmother during the first few years of elementary school, I am far from being a horticulturist. But it appears to me that sometimes we know, simply by looking at them, that our plants need water, light, or some essential nutrient.

Matthew 21:19 illustrates that a tree can live and exist and bear no fruit, but this is not the will of God. Jesus cursed the fig tree because it bore no fruit. The fig tree symbolized the Nation of Israel. Today it could symbolize the Disciples of Christ. Further research provides background that: "the common fig bears the first crop, called the breba crop, meaning 'first fruit,' in the spring on last season's growth. The second crop, known as the primary crop, is born in the fall on the new growth." The absence of a breba crop is an indication that the main crop will not come forth.[29] For this reason, Jesus cursed the fig tree, because it bore no breba. It was a dysfunctional tree.

God had blessed Israel with a desire that certain results be produced to put forth an example of godliness and holiness in the earth through justice, mercy, faithfulness, kindness, meekness, and forgiveness. What we see more prevalently, however, is strife, hatred, rebellion, idolatry, and evil. While revelation is progressive, there is to be

---

29 California Rare Fruit Growers Association, at http://www.crfg.org/pubs/ff/fig.html.

some indication of our commitment to God's will. The illustration of the fig tree that bore no fruit is analogous to those who proclaim to be Christians or believers, but who are ineffective for God's kingdom. There is neither any indication of their light or salt (Matthew 5:13). We are each created with a purpose and are expected to bear fruit to fulfill God's purpose and will on the earth.

The affirmations of true saints are confirmed in Scripture. They are those who have crucified the flesh (Galatians 5:24, 2:20). In his Epistle to the Romans, Paul provides instructions, indicating that there is a reasonable expectation of consecration and conformity to God's will for those who are disciples of Christ. There is a call to offer ourselves as a living sacrifice, holy and acceptable to God (Romans 12:1). It is the "fruit of the Spirit," a biblical term that sums up nine visible attributes of a true Christian life.

Using the King James Version of Galatians 5:22–23, these attributes are love, joy, peace, longsuffering, gentleness, goodness, faith, meekness, and temperance. Again, we learn from Scripture that these are not "individual fruits" from which we pick and choose. Rather, the Fruit of the Spirit is one. It is singular—displaying nine facets of "fruit" that characterize all who truly walk in the Holy Spirit. It is like the body that has many members yet one body (Romans 12:4). Collectively, this is the fruit that all Christians should be producing in their new life.

Dr. William Morris, Founder of Covenant Theological Seminary, stresses that the Fruit of the Spirit emanates from love. Again, love is God's overarching commandment for his disciples. Matthew 22:35–40 describes the first and greatest commandment. That is, we are to love the Lord our God with all of heart, soul, and mind. The second greatest commandment given to God's disciples is to love one's neighbor as one's self. Dr. Morris provides a representation of the fruit of the Spirit contrasted with the temperament of the world. Where the fruit of love abounds, other fruit is manifested. He describes:

Joy is love's strength;
Peace is love's security;
Long-suffering is love's patience;
Gentleness is love's conduct;
Goodness is love's character;
Faith is love's confidence;
Meekness is love's humility; and,
Temperance is love's victory.[30]

While we can dress ourselves each day and adorn ourselves for the most auspicious occasions, the Fruit of the Spirit is not an attribute that we can just put on when we need to display a particular image. There is nothing hidden from God. Psalm 44:21 declares that God searches the heart and knows all its secrets: our thoughts, desires, and planned actions. A person's character is rooted and established in the heart. The heart represents the whole person; who we are, what we are, and how we are. For out of the heart flow the issues of life, whether they be vice or virtue. True conversion and transformation require a genuine and sincere commitment to God and a pure heart.

Transformation is evident. As we previously discussed, sometimes our family or friends refuse to acknowledge that a change has taken place. They remember the old ways, although what they see is the new, transformed person. That transformation also bears witness to others of the power and presence of God in our lives. Sometimes we may not know how that reflection may influence someone in our sphere who desires to be changed or set free in some way. Our reflection does matter. It can make a difference for someone else.

---

[30] Bill Morris Ministries, Inc., Course Syllabus, "Systematic Theology, Covenant Theological Seminary," TH-406.

A Righteous Reflection

Mirror, Mirror:
What Reflection Do You See?

Questions for Thought and Reflection:

1. Am I bearing fruit? If so, what fruit is exhibited through me?

2. What areas have been pruned away?

3. Listening to the Spirit, what areas do I see in my life that will require transforming?

4. What difference am I making in the lives of others?

Chapter 11

The Broken Mirror

The Spirit of the Lord God is upon me;
because the Lord has anointed me
to bring good news to the poor;
he has sent me to bind up the brokenhearted,
to proclaim liberty to the captives,
and the opening of the prison to those who are bound.

—ISAIAH 61:1

Cracked, Broken, or Shattered: Does It Matter?

MIRRORS HAVE LONG held a sense of intrigue and curiosity being the subject of numerous fairytales and folklore. A broken mirror has raised a different kind of reaction. For me, a broken mirror conjures memories of many kinds of superstitions, beliefs and old wives' tales. As a child, I remember how some of my friends, or even adults, would react to a broken mirror. They would "freak out," when they were the cause of a broken mirror. There are numerous books and articles on the subject of mirrors and superstitions, with some even giving you instructions on how to reverse the effects of a broken mirror. I have come to recognize that there is a reason such beliefs are called superstitions. The word superstitious means irrational, unfounded, illogical, and fallacious. Or in other words, there is nothing that has been found to bring validity to the many claims about the mirror, including a broken one.

There is, however, a more obvious fact about a broken mirror. It is just that—the brokenness is apparent to us because we can see it, no question. The severity of the break determines how we might handle it. Some mirrors are completely shattered, with fragments of glass everywhere. If this happens to be the rearview mirror on your vehicle or the only mirror in our home, we may consider that an urgent matter and opt to replace it right away. If there is a slight fracture, a hairline crack that is barely noticeable but broken nonetheless, we might handle it with care and be extra careful, so as not to make it worse. Sometimes a mirror may be cracked but maintain its shape within the frame, or maybe just a corner of the mirror is broken off. Perhaps we kid ourselves, thinking that the mirror will be just fine if it is not handled too much, disregarding any notion that it is just a matter of time before that crack expands, making the mirror useless. We can call these degrees of brokenness but broken nonetheless. Today, it is so amazing to see how fragments of broken mirrors are used in design from furniture, to floors and walls, to picture frames, and so much more. If you can imagine it, then it most likely can be done including a do it yourself project (DIY). People are putting fractured pieces back together again but in unique and different ways.

But what about our internal being, which I will also here refer to as our emotional mirror? It too may be completely shattered from some devastating experience. It may only be cracked or chipped but can still have a significant impact on our growth, our emotional or psychological well-being. It can affect not only our relationships with others but our relationship with God. Are we able to see the state of our internal

The Broken Mirror

mirror as readily as we can see with the natural eye? Perhaps we have not stopped before to consider our internal being and its condition.

Many times, there are some obvious clues showing us that our emotional mirror may be broken. When we are hurt, angry, broken or experience some other negative emotion, it may result in what might appear symbolically as a hairline crack. But left unattended, over time it may grow into a wider fissure. When we harbor ill feelings that turn to bitterness and hate, our emotional mirror needs attention. If there is unforgiveness towards others or even ourselves where we emote self-hatred, our mirror needs care and repair. We know when there is something within us that is unsettled or unresolved. Thoughts may bombard our minds. We may feel agitated and lack peace. We may have a person in our thoughts that is the cause of our anxiety or pain. We may feel like the whole world and everybody is against us and carry a victim mentality. We may have feelings or even do things out of spite or revenge toward another person who had nothing to do with the core issue. Have you ever experienced someone's wrath and wondered what you did to provoke that? Sometimes, it may not have been anything that you did. It may the other person carrying unresolved matters. They become like a steam roller affecting any and everyone in their path, like that erupted volcano we talked about earlier.

There are telltale signs that let us know, something is awry. It is time to face the mirror, as another person or issue has taken control of our emotion and our spiritual well-being. We need to address the matter. Some may say that they are not disturbed because they have dealt with it. I have heard some say that they tucked it far away in the back of the closet and threw away the key. Others say they swept it under the carpet. Well, that is exactly what we discussed earlier. That is, God is constantly cleaning out our internal closet. He sees and knows if a matter has been resolved. He knows when we have tried to put a Band-Aid on it or tried to hide it for life. He knows when the heart is still yet unclean, holding unforgiveness, hate, anger, and a host of other undesirable emotions. Truly, he knows when we have been completely healed or delivered. He knows what is buried deep inside our closet or has been swept under the rug. At some point, he uncovers it for us to face it, confess it and deal with it. Just when we think it is all gone, he uncovers something else. He brings it all to light. He exposes it to us such that we might be completely healed and delivered. There have been many times in my life when I thought that everything that needed to be addressed had been, only to be reminded of something from years ago that wasn't. I can also say that the more a person cleans, that space is replaced with more peace, joy and freedom. It is like God takes out the pain, sorrow, and junk and replaces it with his blessings. He turns "my mourning into dancing and clothed me with gladness," (Psalm 30:11).

While there are many causes of a broken mirror, I have chosen two broad examples of how life events can sometimes unknowingly alter our course and direction in life. Perhaps better stated is that they can derail us and deter us from walking in the path that God has already established for us. Life becomes drudgery and hard. We wonder why. Let's explore these two areas that appear so commonly in the church, our homes, and workplaces.

Injustice

Injustices toward us can shatter our mirror, or it can also in a lesser degree cause minor hairline cracks or any degree between the two. While sin is what **we** do, and we are held accountable, injustices are those actions perpetrated against us. We may have suffered injustices or abuse from childhood into adulthood. There may be experiences that hurt, violated, or changed the direction of our lives. There are emotional, psychological, or physical scars that never healed. Sometimes the victim is harshly judged by family, friends, colleagues, and even the church where they are viewed as being the cause of their own attack.

Judgment from others can be so severe that there is no looking-glass left—just fragments of shattered glass that once stood with such opulence and splendor, casting a clear reflection of its beloved owner.

There are times when we might be able to point to the source of our feelings. We can pinpoint exactly what happened that cracked or shattered our mirror. They are blaring reminders of some past event like divorce, molestation, the sudden death of a spouse, murder, or some other violent act. These injustices include not only physical acts but also emotional trauma and bullying. It could be someone very close and dear to us, being bombarded daily with rejection or betrayal, constant criticism, ridicule or some other attack that causes emotional pain and suffering.

Many carry guilt, unforgiveness and a host of other emotions attached to that horrific event into adulthood. Some think they have tightly tucked away, or suppressed the memories and emotional scars, with every intent to forget. Sometimes these neglected experiences alter God's design in who, how and what we are to be. These experiences, sadly can re-shape our personalities. We have taken on new attributes that God didn't create in us. They form an imposter of how God created us to be. These life experiences shape how we handle conflict. They shape how we react to stressful situations or even casual interactions and relationships with others. They stand in the way of building friendships and trust and can wreak havoc in marriages, families, and even the most casual encounters. What we sometimes may not fully see or understand is just how much our lives have been impacted by these events, but moreover, how much our life is impacted when we try to cover up rather than allow God in.

John 10:10 illustrates this point, reminding us that the thief comes to steal, kill, and to destroy. 1 Peter 5:8, further tells us that we are to be sober-minded and watchful. While we all face some form of a challenge at one point or another over the course of our lifetime, the severity of these life events can change our world, our outlook on life, even our will. Just think how these life experiences have altered that beautiful person whom God has created in you. These experiences have crippled people, where dreams have been cast aside. Challenging experiences derailed some in their life pursuits or exchanged their purpose and calling in life to be an imitator. That is perhaps why we see so many people who are unhappy in their jobs, careers, home, or life, period! Some gave up along the way and just "settled." In many of my discussions with former classmates, I repeatedly hear comments that they do not know how they ended up where they are. They desired to do and be something different.

There are many accounts throughout the Old Testament of how God had a plan for Israel and those he chose for specific purposes. There are examples where it appears that because of circumstances, life changing events took place that set-in motion a new direction. Look at the life of Joseph where God gave him dreams and visions of greatness. Those were glimpses of what God had for him. But the reality is a series of serendipitous situations and injustices that he encountered along the way. He was sold into slavery by his brothers and ended up in Egypt. He was falsely accused by the wife of his master of an inappropriate interaction and was thrown in prison and forgotten for years. He was not, however, forgotten by God who delivered him out of prison and elevated him to the place of his destiny. It was where God designed him to be, a position so high, that only the Pharaoh was above him. But was the process of getting there a part of God's design? What transformation did he undergo while in prison? Did God use that experience to free him of any anger he may have harbored toward his brothers? Was that an experience that was used to take away pride and make him more humble? While there are many questions we may ask about Joseph and why he went through what he did to get to where we know God's plan was ultimately fulfilled We know that God yet prepared him to fulfill the plan he created for Joseph.

Cultural Norms

When we study the character and nature of Christ Jesus, it is clear that He loves all. In His Word, He says, "Those who are well have no need of a physician, but those who are sick. I came not to call the righteous, but sinners" (Mark 2:17). But we all have sinned and fallen short of God's glory (Romans 3:23). As we have discussed, there are many kinds of experiences and injustices that may damage our mirror. But perhaps unknowingly, they create patterns in our lives. That is, we become accustomed to doing things a particular way or, we react to some things a certain way. It is like when Israel came out of Egypt and free from slavery, bondage, and oppression. When things were hard in the desert, however, they desired to return to Egypt because they remembered the abundance and diversity of food. They remembered having houses, no matter how humble that shelter may have been. They failed to see that God had positioned them for so much more. They did not want to let go of the patterns that were deeply ingrained in their emotions regardless of the compounded injustices of slavery that they had experienced. Although they had escaped bondage, slavery, and oppression, the people yet rationalized that Egypt was better and longed to return. Our Savior is ready to intervene to not only free us from the injustices but also from customs, and traditions that may cloud our mirror and hinder our oneness with Christ.

In His earthly ministry, Jesus defied the cultural norms of His day. He reached those who were marginalized and considered to be the social outcasts of society. Jesus's path took Him to the woman at the well. "The Samaritan woman said to Him, 'How is it that you, a Jew, ask for a drink from me, a woman of Samaria?'" (John 4:9).

Jesus's actions violated cultural norms. The Samaritans were outcasts of society. The Jews of Jerusalem vehemently despised them. The rift between the Jews and Samaritans dates back in Israel's history to approximately 930 BC, the time of the divided kingdom of the Jews, when the northern kingdom was referred to as Israel and the southern kingdom, Judah. During the Assyrian captivity, the people intermingled with pagan nations and became a mixed race, which was contrary to Jewish traditions.

The day Jesus met the Samaritan woman, when the disciples eventually caught up with their Lord, after being apart from Him in their journey, they were shocked to find Him engaged in conversation with a Samaritan woman. You can perhaps envision the whispering and the quiet discussions among themselves. In their minds, they may have questioned, "Why is our Lord talking with this outcast of society? Doesn't He know who this woman is?" Jesus could have taken a different path. He could also have drunk water from the well and continued His way without any personal interaction. But His encounter was life-changing to the woman, as He took time to engage in discussion with her and provide spiritual water. Her brief encounter with Jesus had a lifelong impact, not only on her but on others in her community who heard the testimony and went to the well, hoping to have a similar encounter. For the Samaritan woman, it was perhaps like being given a new mirror to see her true reflection and the beauty of Christ Jesus within. Whether your healing or deliverance has been impacted by cultural norms of how you are expected to react, behave or overcome, or new norms where you have just grown so accustomed to your way of life you have come to believe that it is your destiny, know that Christ is he who defies the norm.

Pride

I woke up this morning thinking about the broken mirror. I then began to realize that we are all really born with a flawed if not broken mirror. Romans 5:8 tells that that, "sin came into the world through one man, and death through sin, and so death spread to all men because all sinned…" Romans 3:23 also tells us that, "for all have sinned and fall short of the glory of God." We have all sinned and we are all born into sin having a sin nature. As we dwell in these imperfect bodies of earthen clay, we are hindered from reaching the highest level of perfection. However, the apostle Paul speaks clearly that this does not give us cause to continually and deliberately sin. Paul affirms throughout his epistles to the church that we must be transformed: Transformed from a sin and unregenerate nature into a Christ-like nature. It is a progressive walk. As we mature in our relationship with Christ, we are to reflect an image and likeness of Christ Jesus.

But sometimes we fall way short of that mark because we are not perfect in these earthen bodies. At times we may stumble and fall short. Yes, I have had my share, and I still do stumble. I hope it is refreshing to know that this book is not to exclaim the self-righteous, as though any of us have arrived at a state of perfection. But merely, it is an exhortation that we can all face the mirror and see for ourselves who, what, and how we are. When we are focused on taking inventory of ourselves, it certainly diminishes our ability to point a finger and criticize or judge others. However, pride is that giant elephant that refuses to see the truth, face truth, or acknowledge truth. Pride is that attitude that says, "not me; it's you." Pride is deceitful because it keeps you from seeing yourself. It is dangerous because it causes you to believe a lie rather than truth. Pride will fill you with arrogance such that you don't or won't listen to wise counsel. Pride steals your humility and will have you believe that you are always right. Pride is a destructive spirit that keeps you from experiencing God's best and God's destiny for your life. It is a belligerent attitude of doing it your way.

An overarching message here is that God sees in us more than what we see in the natural mirror. My aim is that this book will help readers see beyond the physical realm to experience what God sees in His creation of us, and the beauty that He has created within us. Psalm 139 says that "we are fearfully and wonderfully made." Just know that when we are in the midst of sin, brokenness, or pride, we can always go back to our foundation of how God created us. There also lies His healing virtue. We all have an opportunity to be transformed as Disciples of Christ Jesus, bearing fruit and impacting our world in a greater way. We, however, must trust and believe and provide a response to the gift God has given to us. What is this gift? It is the gift of Salvation.

Salvation

One of the first Bible verses I remember memorizing is John 3:16, "For God so loved the world, that he gave his only begotten Son, that whosoever believeth in Him should not perish, but have everlasting life" (KJV). God made provision for us to be restored to a right relationship with Him through His Son Jesus. Through Jesus' sacrificial act on the cross, he became the propitiation for our sin. As I previously mentioned, the Apostle Paul's teaching in the Book of Romans reveals how the sins of one man, Adam, caused all to become sinners. Further, through the righteous act of one Man, Jesus Christ, many will be made righteous. He further expounds that, where sin increased, grace abounded more, including the effects of sin against us. We are overcomers through Christ Jesus.

However, salvation has a more holistic perspective throughout Scripture. Salvation is seen throughout the biblical text from the book of Genesis to Revelation. "Broadly speaking, one might say that salvation is the overriding theme of the entire Bible ... It is a multi-dimensional subject with a broad range of meanings."[31] Salvation is seen throughout Scripture as humankind's relationship with God, man's relationship with man, man's relationship with nature with a holistic emphasis on health, healing, and wellness. This relationship includes physical security, protection, and prosperity in all aspects of life, not just financial.

---

31 William T. Arnold, "Salvation," in Walter Elwell, ed., *Baker's Evangelical Dictionary of Biblical Theology*, at
http://www.biblestudytools.com/dictionary/salvation/.

"While the New Testament emphasizes the spiritual elements of salvation, the Old Testament sees salvation from God as more physical than spiritual, and more social than individual. For example, Joseph's rise to fame in Egypt preserves the lives of his entire family (Gen 45:4–7). Through Noah's faithfulness, God brings salvation to his family as well as animal life (Gen. 7–9). And the blessing of the promise of nationhood and land for Abraham was not only for his descendants but all families on the earth (Gen 12:1–3). After 430 years in Egypt, an entire people is delivered through Moses (Exod. 1–12). Through Esther's rise to power, the Jewish people are spared annihilation (Esther 7)."[32]

All throughout the Old Testament, salvation from God is predominant. It is he who fights our battles (Deuteronomy 3:21). He delivers us out of all our troubles" (Psalm 34:17). It is God who protects us (Isaiah 54:17). While these are just a few examples, it is evident from the Old Testament alone that God is constant in our lives. He is always present and concerned about every aspect of life including our spiritual condition. When Israel strayed, God in His infinite mercy sent the prophets to sound the alarm to bring the people to repentance from their sinful ways and return to Him and His covenant, which provided for their well-being in every aspect of life.

The theme of salvation with an emphasis on one's spiritual well-being and transformation from a sinful nature is seen throughout the New Testament. The root of sin is a sinful nature. It is when we are born again that enables us to receive a new transformed nature including deliverance from the effects of sin. God wants us all to grow and thrive. Second Peter 3:18 instructs, "But grow in the grace and knowledge of our Lord and Savior Jesus Christ." There are so many who are hindered in their growth because of the factors discussed in this writing. It is difficult to advance and move forward if you are constantly, or even periodically, holding onto past experiences, sorrow, pain, unforgiveness,

---
32 Ibid.

or non-biblical worldview philosophies, beliefs, or understandings. It is impossible to move forward if you are hanging onto the old nature. "If anyone is in Christ, he is a new creation. The old has passed away; behold, the new has come" (2 Corinthians 5:17). Can you imagine driving a car while constantly looking in the rearview mirror?

Whatever sin was committed in the past, or whatever egregious action you have experienced, the good news is that when you elect to make Jesus Christ, Lord, and Savior, the transforming work begins to bring about healing, restoration, deliverance, and wholeness. In the Old Testament, Isaiah 43:25, the Lord God speaks, "I am he who blots out your transgressions for my own sake, and I will not remember your sins." We are given a new beginning, like starting a new year, fresh, without blot, spot, or wrinkle. Though our friends and family may recall our past and may even try to bring it up, we have confidence in the Lord that we are set free. We can face the mirror and look in a brand-new mirror because we put our trust in God.

The more we study the biblical text and walk in obedience, the more we can make a self-assessment. The more we submit our will to God's will, the more we are transformed. I like how Bible Study Tools.com says that "Where individuals are singled out it seems to be for the good of the community. For example, the Genesis narrative develops the theme of God's blessing, which though resting on certain individuals, renders them agents for some greater work of God."[33] God's desire is to transform us to be more like Him. He also holds the vision, the master plan, and purpose for our existence. He wants to prepare us for his purpose. "Eye has not seen, nor ear heard, nor have entered into the heart of man the things which God has prepared for those who love him" (1 Corinthians 2:9 NKJV). This transformation process is not a destination but rather a process. It is a growing relationship with God every day.

---

33 Ibid.

The Broken Mirror

A Like New Mirror: R^3—Revival, Restoration, Rejuvenation

Perhaps you have reached this point and concluded that your mirror is not broken, nor has it ever been broken or even cracked. If that is you, then read on. Sometimes the mirror may not be broken or cracked, but perhaps the reflection has been significantly diminished or made dull. Our mirror may be tarnished, cloudy, or just plain dirty from neglect and careful attention. This may be an indication that our focus is on everything but God. We may be in a "fog" or on automatic pilot. We get so accustomed to a routine that it becomes a ritual. Like Monday through Friday—we get up by 7:00 a.m. We have our morning cup of coffee and maybe a light breakfast. We quickly read our daily devotional and newspaper. We offer a quick prayer, get dressed, and head off to work. We return home, play with the kids and talk about their day, help with dinner, dishes, and homework, watch TV, have a short conversation with the spouse, and go to bed. After only a few short months, this kind or repeated activity and routine can become so ritualistic that you don't think about it anymore, you just do it.

I recall while working in Washington, DC, taking the same route to work every day. One morning, I pulled out of the garage in my northern Virginia home and headed to work as usual. With traffic being light that morning, about twenty minutes later, I pulled into a parking space in the garage at my office. Just as I was about to exit my car, I stopped and thought about my drive that morning. It was a blur! I did not recall any of the sights along the way. I did not recall cars that I passed along the way, or the people, or how the weather appeared. I had just driven for twenty minutes on automatic pilot, oblivious to all my surroundings. We go through life on automatic pilot—until one day, we realize that we are just exhausted and worn out. The mundaneness of life has worn away our zeal and zest for life. Instead of looking at each morning as a new day with excitement and anticipation, it becomes drudgery and just another day.

I also recall my routine meetings with federal agencies. On a memorable occasion, I met a colleague from the Pennsylvania office who came to DC for meetings we attended together. We took a taxi from our office to the federal agency, arriving very early. Instead of waiting in the lobby of the building, as I had done on many occasions before, he suggested that we walk across the street to a garden in front of one of the Smithsonian museums. I reluctantly agreed. As we crossed the street, I observed the museum with its garden of flowers in front. They were in full bloom, and the aroma filled the air. I noticed the park benches along the walkway leading into the museum. We found and sat on an empty one. He again suggested that we could just sit there in the garden for a few minutes until it was time to head back across the street for our meeting. I thought how crazy it was. We had a very important meeting with this federal agency. We'd been working for months discussing a partnership to conduct a multimillion-dollar research project, and he wanted to sit in the park and smell the roses. I thought how I should have his job if he had so much time even to suggest such a thing.

As these thoughts continued to bombard my mind, I noticed he wasn't talking. He didn't glance at his notes. He just sat there soaking in the gentle rays of sun, the aroma of the flowers, enjoying the moment. I then began to reflect on my own life and how I would have stayed in the federal building, sat in the lobby, studied my notes over and over and over again until time for my meeting. I would have left promptly after my meeting ended, jumped into a taxi, and gone directly back to my office to continue the grind. It was embarrassing to me that as many times as I had been to that agency for meetings, I had never even noticed the museum across the street. I had never seen the beautiful garden filled with assorted flowers or the park benches. It was an example of how we go through life and—that ole' cliché— we never stop to "smell the roses."

Well, I quickly faced the mirror that time and captured that fundamental lesson of learning to smell the roses along the pathways of life. In fact, today, I sometimes must face the mirror to ensure that I am not overdoing it. Being in business for myself the past few years has afforded me an opportunity and the flexibility to do so many things I have wanted to do in the past, but work schedules and priorities stood in the way. I can play tennis or golf during the day or go to the gym. I can join the lady's guild at church for morning Bible studies, brunches, or meet friends for lunch at odd hours. There are so many other things I am able to accomplish, including writing this book, because of more flexibility with my schedule.

But no matter if you are in the workplace, a stay-at-home parent or spouse, or are self-employed, take time to face the mirror. Determine whether you have slipped into automatic pilot and just left the "controls" there. You may need to go into manual mode from time to time to stay fully engaged with what's going on today. We need to ensure that our time with God is not on autopilot and zeal is not being suppressed and reduced to a daily ritual.

Whether your mirror has been broken, shattered, cloudy, or is just plain dirty, Christ is the great Physician, Healer, and Restorer. He is the One who brings revival, restoration, and rejuvenation. These three words are synonymous, meaning to bring alive again. It denotes that there was life, and something happened to diminish that life. But Christ is able not only to restore that life, but to ensure that God's divine plan, purpose, and will are being fulfilled. Restoring our zeal in the things of Christ enables us to persevere, overcome, prosper, and thrive in our relationship with Him, our family, and our community. It is what makes our mirror sparkle and shine with vibrancy.

Mirror, Mirror:
What Reflection Do You See?

Questions for Thought and Reflection:

1. What condition is your mirror in, broken, shattered, cloudy, dull, or just plain dirty?

2. What do you need to do to restore its sparkle and clarity?

3. A person has been hurt and abused and has carried a victim's mentality for many years. Though you recently met, you too are blamed for their problem and life disappointments. What is your response?

4. What changes can you make concerning cultural influences or realizing you accepted a new norm in your life that could open up some new experiences for you in a Biblical Worldview perspective?

Chapter 12

Be All In

Whoever is not with me is against me, and whoever does not gather with me scatters.
—LUKE 11:23

A Full Immersion Is Required

DURING THEIR PRETEEN years, I enrolled both of my daughters in swimming classes at the Y. They were quite enthusiastic. After each class, over dinner, they would share highlights of the lesson and the things they had accomplished. The report from my younger daughter was always very terse, with not much to report except that she got in the water. Then one day, she was more excited about her achievement. The teacher also seemed to be quite pleased, so I couldn't wait to hear the details. As customary, over dinner, I received her report: after about four weeks, she had finally put her head underwater. She was all in, from head to toe, fully immersed. Well, that was quite an accomplishment! While it may appear "cute" on the surface, as her mother, I could only lament that she'd inherited my genes. I too had taken swimming lessons as a preteen; while I did stick my head underwater on the first day, I excused myself from the class when the coach took everyone down to the other end of the pool with ten feet of water and expected us to jump in.

I share this story because it is reminding me of some observations I've had through the years. Through the chapters of this book, we have discussed the mirror, its reflection, and the various aspects of assessing ourselves and the standard of measurement and more. The final point in this writing is that being a Christian or a disciple of Jesus Christ, depending on your preferred terminology, requires a full commitment. We must be "all in." In today's world, where there is an ever-increasing push toward being "tolerant," some have backed away and taken a very "cold" approach to Christianity. Some are afraid of open expression of their faith for fear of insulting others or appearing less than tolerant. A huge part of having a sound spiritual mirror is so that others may see Christ through us. While we are always to be ready to share our faith, scripture tells us we are to "be" witnesses. That is before any word is spoken, they can see some attributes of Godly character, moral values, dignity and love.

Inside and Outside

"Ye are the salt of the earth: but if the salt has lost his savor, wherewith shall it be salted? It is thenceforth good for nothing, but to be cast out, and to be trodden under foot of men. Ye are the light of the world. A city that is set on a hill cannot be hid. Neither do men light a candle, and put it under a bushel, but on a candlestick; and it giveth light unto all that are in the house. Let your light so shine before men, that they may see your good works, and glorify your Father which is in heaven" (Matthew 5:13–16 KJV).

We are called to both be witnesses and to be ready to share with others when we have an opportunity to do so. There is to be an outward manifestation by vivid actions to show forth the heart of the person. Being aligned with Christ starts within and then radiates into outward actions. Having care and compassion for the poor and oppressed, helping those who are sick or going through tough times are a few ways. Rather than point to excuses or reasons why people endure what they endure, without judgment, we do what we can do to help.

We are called to have a visible and active presence in the world and to have impact in our homes, workplaces, and communities. As Paul says, the race is not to the swift, but to the one who completes it. Getting to the finish line requires a commitment to God's will. It requires perseverance such that we become "steadfast, immovable, always abounding in the work of the Lord, knowing that in the Lord your labor is not in vain" (1 Corinthians 15:58).

Spiritual growth, as we have seen, is progressive. It is a process of transformation that leads us to spiritual maturity day by day, which cannot be achieved without understanding and a consistent application of the virtues of Scripture. The more we apply what we learn, the more we mature in our relationship with God. The more we mature, the more we cast a reflection that embodies the nature and likeness of Christ. The more we cast a reflection in the image of Christ, the more impact we have in our homes, community, church, and the world—wherever God may lead us. We can have impact when God uses us to minister to others or speak, teach, or preach. We have impact in our professions and with the people we encounter. We can have impact and influence within the political realm to promote laws that are for the good of society, not for selfish motives or vain ambitions. We uplift those we may encounter, even in the direst of situations. We infuse hope in the lives of the oppressed because we are filled with compassion. We are less focused on self and the everyday cares of life, and more focused on the well-being of others. We rise above the ordinary, day-to-day concerns, knowing that God is ever faithful in taking care of our needs such that we can focus on caring for others.

The parable of the sower in Luke 8:5–15 provides a test that can help make a further assessment of ourselves in our progress toward a transformed life. This transformed life can come only from a continual growth in our relationship with God.

> *"A sower went out to sow his seed. And as he sowed, some fell along the path and was trampled underfoot, and the birds of the air devoured it. And some fell on the rock, and as it grew up, it withered away, because it had no moisture. And some fell among thorns, and the thorns grew up with it and choked it. And some fell into good soil and grew and yielded a hundredfold…* "*Now the parable is this: The seed is the word of God. The ones along the path are those who have heard; then the devil comes and takes away the word from their hearts, so that they may not believe and be saved. And the ones on the rock are those who, when they hear the word, receive it with joy. But these have no root; they believe for a while, and in time of testing fall away. And as for what fell among the thorns, they are those who hear, but as they go on their way they are choked by the cares and riches and pleasures of life, and their fruit does not mature. As for that in the good soil, they are those who, hearing the word, hold it fast in an honest and good heart, and bear fruit with patience."*

We are likewise instructed to be conformed to His image so that we, too, may draw others to Christ by the light of God that we carry within and so that we may be the salt of the earth (Matthew 5:13). If we are sitting on the fence in a lukewarm state, or perhaps seen as having one foot in Christ and one foot in the world, we have no impact, just as salt that loses its savor is useless. I am one who enjoys good food that is well seasoned with real salt, herbs, and a variety of fresh spices. But if that salt does not add flavor to the food, then it is left on the shelf or replaced by some alternative.

God doesn't do a phenomenal job in transforming your life to keep it then hidden and tucked away. Rather, He has prepared to send you out to have impact in the world. Your world may not be global in a geographic sense. It may be your family where you provide light and encouragement. It may be your hometown community. For others, it may be a wider territory. But wherever your mission field may be, there is a great need for those whose life and lifestyle epitomizes a transformed life. That transformed life is one that is relevant, thought-provoking, life-transforming, and has impact. Life is no longer just about us, but we have a sincere desire to effect change in our homes, communities, our nation, and the world for the betterment of people. We have greater compassion for others, though we may not understand their paths, the oppression or discrimination they have experienced, the struggles they encounter, or why things are the way they are. But we can see a glimpse of God's love and compassion to do what we can do to make it better for someone else.

There are so many opportunities to make a difference that we could become overwhelmed. But in the transformational process, I believe that God is also honing our gifts, talents, and abilities. He is grooming us in ways that will enable us to (1) recognize where we have a passion for making a difference and (2) equip us to be effective.

Making an impact is both spiritual and practical (Acts 9:32–43). Yes! We can do so much to change the world. It won't happen, however, just by the positions we hold, unless God put us in these positions to make an impact. It won't be by the financial wealth we have unless God gave us the finances to use for building His kingdom. You can't just throw money at something and expect it to be solved. There are ongoing US-government-funded programs that have shown little to no success but continue to receive federal funding. Neither will it happen by our talents and abilities, unless God gave us those gifts and talents and we are using them according to His will. Regardless of our gifts, talents, abilities, wealth or the lack thereof, or positions, first and foremost we are compelled to living a life that reflects Christ Jesus. Having impact that reaches far beyond our mere human and individual capability begins with how we live each and every day. It is about the reflection that we cast.

Fruit and Influence

God is sovereign and has not only given but allows us to exercise free will in life. Although we have a free will to choose, God loves us and desires that we will each choose to serve Him—not out of obligation or fear—but that we will reciprocate the love that He has poured out over us by sharing it with others. God desires that we have a fruitful and prosperous life here on the earth knowing that He is the source of all that we have and all that we are. God affirms who He is through his written Word, the biblical text, and also through the gift of His Son Jesus, the Christ.

As mature saints of God, we have more influence because, though we may not always be able to speak a word, others can see "something different." We are known by the fruit we bear, love, joy, peace, patience, kindness, goodness, faithfulness, gentleness, and self-control. There are many whose paths we cross and who observe us from afar. American poet Edgar Guest wrote about a sermon he would rather see than hear. Imagine the power and impact of messaging though no word is spoken?

Isn't it time? Isn't it time that we, as Disciples of Christ, begin to cast a reflection that is aligned with the words that we speak? Isn't it time that we come to a place of casting away judgment of others and face the mirror for ourselves? Isn't it time that we seek the will of God in our lives, recognizing that the *vox populi* is only evanescent and filled with vain hope? Isn't it time we recognize that there is only one righteous standard: Jesus Christ our Lord and that, as Disciples of Christ, isn't it time that we cast a reflection of his nature, character, and spirit? Isn't it time?

Mirror, Mirror:
What Reflection Do You See?

Questions for Thought and Reflection:

1. If I never speak a word, what does my life speak about me?

2. More importantly, what does my life say to God? Am I all in, or do I only want three dollars' worth?

3. Am I all in, or do I only seek the *vox populi*?

4. Am I all in, seeking the glory and goodness of God in my life for a full and complete transformation into a disciple worthy of my calling?

Chapter 13

The New Norm: Exposed

A Closing Testimony

SOMETIMES WE FACE the mirror with sincere intentions, but again we may unknowingly face a dull and cloudy mirror. Without a clear mirror, we may only see bits and pieces of the full picture. We may only see surface deep and don't get a full understanding of what is deeply embedded. These factors and others may hinder us from getting to the root cause and origin. Then there may also be times when we dismiss what we do see, surmising that they are insignificant, or harmless because they have always been there. We have come to accept some things as "just a normal way of life." I need to repeat this, "we have come to accept some things in our life as just a normal way of life." It is what some now call, a "New Normal."

I attended a Prayer Conference this past weekend in Atlanta, Georgia. As I drove from Tallahassee, Florida to Atlanta, my prayer was that I not return home in the same way. I'm not talking about the geographic route, but about my state of mind, my emotional IQ, and my physical well-being. Over the past several months, I have felt an increase of burdens in my life. I have been a caregiver for Mother

Clarice, a support for my dad, my children, other family members and friends who call upon me to pray for them and their heaviness. I have carried my own weights of managing a business, completing a book, and other personal matters. Living in the house with Mother Clarice brought comfort and friendship. With her transition, I have experienced loneliness, feelings of anxiety and fear. This is not the Adriene I know. So, I welcomed prayer for myself and for my home. Little did I know what was in store for me.

As I arrived and sat in the sanctuary, the conference director spoke about the agenda and the weekend ahead of us. She talked about the dynamic speakers, and some breakout rooms where there was a chiropractor offering her services, and a deliverance room for those experiencing addictions or abuse. Well, I quickly surmised that I would not go to either of those sessions. I had received the services of a chiropractor after a car accident several years ago and did not care for the technique that was used. I recalled jerking and popping of joints. No thank you! While I didn't think her description of those needing deliverance applied to me, I couldn't also negate my perceptions about deliverance ministries. Anytime someone mentioned "deliverance," my memories would take me back to my high school days. I remember many of my classmates attended Revival services at a neighborhood holiness church. While they would come to school and share stories of what they witnessed at the revival services, it appeared to me that many, if not all, tried to understand what was happening. They described in detail about people shouting, hollering, and some rolling on the floor. My friends and I were intrigued by the stories and many of them attended the remaining revival services. I don't know if they went to get deliverance or if they wanted to see for themselves what transpired. Although I was curious, I respectfully declined. Although I personally saw a change in some of my classmates that attended, I developed an adverse mindset about deliverance services. Throughout my Christian life, anytime I would hear the word, "deliverance," I would steer clear and go the other way. That may have been a cloudy area in my mirror, but perhaps it was time for the mirror to clear up. It is like when I get in my car sometimes in the morning and my mirror is foggy. When I turn on the defroster, the condensation begins to clear up and you can see the frost being melted away. It is hard to drive with a foggy windshield but some of us try to do it anyway.

A New Normal: Exposed

Sometimes, we need to be delivered from our mindsets. Sometimes we need to be delivered from things that we have been misinformed about, or not informed about at all. There are times when we carry emotional weights, psychological distortions, distorted memories, deep-seated feelings, and other attachments that causes us to adopt a new way of life and a new way of thinking. This is what has come to be known as, "The New Normal." It has been a way of life for so long, we think this is the way it is, the way it is supposed to be, or this is our lot in life.

Sometimes, we don't even recognize that we have a new normal. It is like a train track. The rails on a track may have switches. Switches are necessary to control traffic. They can enable a train to move seamlessly from one track to another, change the direction of the train, or stall the train to allow other trains to pass.[34] You may not even realize that the train has switched from one track to another, but when you disembark, you will quickly know if that is not your intended destination.

I am here declaring that this "New Normal" can be a deceptive imposter. While we can overcome some great deficiencies in our lives and develop a new norm, it can also be a silently placed alternate pathway in life. It was setup by some traumatic event or action that changed our God-given make-up and our direction. While a train is generally

---

34 Craig Freudenrich, Ph.D., *How Trains Work*, https://science.howstuffworks.com/transport/engines-equipment/train2.htm

switched deliberately from one track to another, our course in life may also have been intentionally altered as a plan of the enemy to derail what God has for us. We have been living life on a path that God did not ordain, anoint, or establish for us. Perhaps our track did not change. We may be on the right track but not progressing as God had intended. Somewhere on our track in life, we got shifted, decelerated, or stalled. Have you ever sat at a railroad crossing waiting to pass while the train just sat there blocking the crossing? It didn't move forward or backwards. It just sat there. Or maybe it moved forward and few yards, stopped and then backed up a few yards and repeated this exercise several times while you sat there in your car waiting to cross that railroad track. It reminds me of the idiom, "take three steps forward and get pushed two steps back." The reality of what we see is that we make progress that builds excitement and hope of victory that is quickly eradicated by setbacks, disappointments, or difficulties. The constancy of this reality can diminish our hope to a place where we begin to accept life the way it is, and we begin to live that life.

God did not give us a new norm. He created us from the very beginning with a plan and a purpose in mind. This is clearly stated in Jeremiah 29:11-13 which says, *"For I know the plans I have for you, declares the Lord, plans for welfare and not for evil, to give you a future and a hope.* [12] *Then you will call upon me and come and pray to me, and I will hear you.* [13] *You will seek me and find me, when you seek me with all your heart."* God constantly draws us to him. When things spin out of control, when we are weary from the weights, burdens, and the cares of life begin to compound, He invites us to cast them all on Him. It is however, an action on our part. We must act. Hebrews 11:6 tells us that, *"Without faith it is impossible to please him, for whoever would draw near to God must believe that he exists and that he rewards those who seek him."* God wants to bless us. He wants us to prosper us and He wants us to be in health, but we must have faith, and we must seek Him.

The New Norm: Exposed

Something is Awry

It was day two at the prayer conference and the leader again shared the agenda for the day. She talked about the speakers and the esteemed guests. She reminded the participants of the breakout rooms and the services available including the chiropractor and the deliverance team. This time, she specified that if there were any present who might be experiencing grief, anxiety or just overwhelmed, that they might want to check out the deliverance session and meet with the counselors. At that moment, hearing this new set of criteria that connected with my reality: anxiety, grief, and fear, I realized that the Holy Spirit was moving me beyond my perceptions of "deliverance" and getting my attention. I felt a melting taking place. Before that time, I would never have even contemplated going to a deliverance session. But because I clearly connected with the description she cited, I thought that perhaps it was worth checking out. I thought too about my prayer to not return home in the same condition in which I came. I was facing my mirror and though I could not see clearly all that was there, I did not like what I could see and feel. I wanted better. I knew that I wanted freedom. My first step was one of recognition that something was awry and needed to be addressed. My second step was a bold move of faith. I signed up for the deliverance session.

I showed up for my scheduled time, not knowing what to expect. The session was a one-on-one with three awesome women of God including a professional counselor out of Denver, Colorado, a doctor from Atlanta, GA, and a woman with a spiritual gift of discernment from Redford, MI. My session which should have lasted thirty minutes, lasted three hours. These counselors left no stone unturned. While I went in for a few observations I had of myself, they felt led to explore my life beginning with my childhood and upbringing. They explored events that happened in my upbringing being raised for a few years by my grandmother. They explored my marital life, divorce, and relationships with parents, children, and siblings. They were constantly identifying emotional and psychological factors that shaped my life in an unintended way. They also connected the dots with what happened in the past to behavioral indications today as an adult woman. It was like God opening many doors from my past and cleaning out junk. I spoke earlier about how God is constantly cleaning out and that transformation is a lifelong journey. Just when we might think that there is nothing more to shed, God opens a new door and reveals "stuff." In my case, these new doors opened to years of collected junk that I didn't know existed. It's like when I clean my wardrobe and find clothes that I have no idea of where they came from, or I had forgotten that they were there. I have vowed to myself that I will explore my own closet before buying new outfits. I always find something new or barely used.

As we continued to explore deeper and deeper about my past life, I began to see how some experiences I encountered created emotions that have never been dealt with. They were compressed, and other emotions added on top. I have harbored them for most of my life. The counselors identified abandonment, rejection, and emotional and verbal abuse, that led to other factors like fear, trauma, loneliness, and numbness. Can you imagine how these, and other factors can cause a person's life to be reshaped from God's original design. It doesn't mean that there were not accomplishments, to the contrary. It doesn't necessarily mean that my life has been dysfunctional life. In my case, it was the opposite. There have been many accomplishments and drive, but with a drive to overcompensate for fear of failure. These factors drove me to work harder, to strive for perfection, and perhaps take a prideful stance that I will not fail. It was an, "I can do it myself" mentality instead of casting my cares upon the Lord who cares for me.

A Reclaimed Life

I am forever grateful to God for choosing His vessels and placing the three of them on a divine assignment to minister to me. They led me by the Holy Spirit into releasing long-held adverse emotions, characteristic of the "new norm," and assuring deliverance. I am free and no longer bound to unauthorized or unsuspecting attributes. The deception in this new normal is that it exists in a way that causes us to accept it as who, what and how we are. We think that this is just the way we are, or this is the way it is to be. We surrender and indifferently declare it to be our New Normal.

I now know what it is to be free, to be delivered. I am the person God created me to be, not an imposter. My outlook on life is better defined. It is clear and bright. The emotions I described are gone. The atmosphere in my home is changed. Other people around me are commenting about the change they see and how they can see it and hear it in my voice. I have reclaimed my life and the life God purposed for me from the beginning. It is a place of total fulfillment. I am reminded of the word in Proverbs 10:22 that says, *"The blessing of the Lord makes rich, and he adds no sorrow with it."* I am ready for new heights and greater dimensions in Christ. Are you?

Mirror, Mirror:
What Reflection Do You See?

Questions for Thought and Reflection:

1. Are you willing to face the mirror and allow God to do a transformative work in your life?

2. Are there some things that you know about that need to be dealt with? Do you see a cloudy mirror and think there may be other "stuff" that you are not aware of?

3. What New Normal experiences or emotions can you identify?

4. Are you willing to settle, or do you want all that God purposed for your life?

www.ingramcontent.com/pod-product-compliance
Lightning Source LLC
Chambersburg PA
CBHW070601010526
44118CB00012B/1409